ACCLAIM FOR
MERCY'S GAZE

In these anxious times, in which no one seems to be able to sit still for any length of time and in which there is the ever present temptation to check one's smartphone, Vinny Flynn has given us the antidote! In this deceptively simple book, Vinny reminds us of our Lord's invitation to gaze upon His image — just as Jesus had asked of St. Faustina when He appeared to her and then told her to have His image painted. Vinny invites us in a very manageable, practical way to contemplate passages from the Sacred Scriptures, together with closely related passages from St. Faustina's *Diary*. We can then gaze upon the Divine Mercy Image, so that the Lord can heal our hearts as we center our lives on Him! I highly recommend *Mercy's Gaze*, which is really a prayer book that can be brought with you wherever you go.

— **Fr. Joseph G. Roesch, MIC**
Vicar General, Congregation of Marians

Mercy's Gaze

100 Readings
from Scripture *and*
the Diary of St. Faustina

Vinny Flynn
Author of *7 Secrets of the Eucharist*

Foreword and Theme Reflections by
David C. Came

MARIAN PRESS
STOCKBRIDGE MA 01263

2013

Available from:
Marian Helpers Center
Stockbridge, MA 01263

Prayerline: 1-800-804-3823
Orderline: 1-800-462-7426
Website: www.marian.org

Imprimi Potest:
Very Rev. Kazimierz Chwalek, MIC
Provincial Superior
The Blessed Virgin Mary, Mother of Mercy Province
September 21, 2013

ISBN: 978-1-59614-291-6

Cover Art: The restored Vilnius Divine Mercy Image, copyright ©
Marian Fathers of the Immaculate Conception of the B.V.M.

Design of Cover and Pages: Kathy Szpak
Editing and Proofreading:
David Came, Erin Flynn, Andrew Leeco, and Chris Sparks

Nihil Obstat:
Lector Officialis
Most Rev. George H. Pearce, SNM

Imprimatur:
Most Rev. Joseph F. Maguire
Bishop of Springfield, Mass.
January 29, 1988

Printed in the United States of America

DEDICATION

To **Fr. George W. Kosicki, CSB,**
who has mirrored for me the
Merciful Gaze of God.

Table of Contents

FOREWORD

It's a great privilege and joy to write the Foreword to *Mercy's Gaze: 100 Readings from Scripture and the Diary of St. Faustina* by Vinny Flynn.

There are two main reasons why it's such a privilege and joy. The first is my admiration and respect for Vinny's many important contributions to promoting the Divine Mercy message and devotion, especially as a writer and an editor. These contributions include helping the Marian Fathers edit the English edition of the *Diary of St. Faustina* as well as co-authoring two masterworks on Divine Mercy that have been in print for many years and have appeared in various Marian Press editions: *The Divine Mercy Message and Devotion* and *Now Is the Time for Mercy*.

Vinny also served for seven years as editor of *The Association of Marian Helpers BULLETIN* (now *Marian Helper* magazine). This magazine is one of the primary publications in the world that covers the Divine Mercy movement in the life of the Church.

'A PARTICULAR GOSPEL OF DIVINE MERCY'

The second reason I'm overjoyed to write the Foreword is because this book breaks new ground in making the case that the *Diary of St. Faustina* as private revelation stacks up well against the yardstick of the inspired Word of God in Sacred Scripture.

In this regard, Vinny has gone far beyond producing another thematic treasury of passages from the *Diary*. Guided by his deep knowledge of Divine Mercy, he has painstakingly mined parallel passages from Scripture and the *Diary* that develop key mercy themes, as well as themes common to the

Christian life. The result is not only rich spiritual fare for prayer and reflection on God's mercy, but confirmation of the *Diary's* consistency and harmony with Scripture. Set alongside Scripture, St. Faustina's revelations come alive as a striking Gospel of Mercy intended for our time.

Further, just as all of Scripture ultimately points to Jesus Christ as its fulfillment, so Vinny frames all of his readings with a call for the reader to gaze upon and return the gaze of the crucified and risen Lord Jesus — as depicted in the Divine Mercy Image that was revealed to St. Faustina. The goal of such double or mutual gazing, as the author puts it, is our transformation into living images of mercy. (Read Vinny's masterful explanation of this in the Introduction.)

But don't just take my word for this assessment of *Mercy's Gaze*. Consider the remarkable words of Pope John Paul II in his last book, published in 2005. It's almost as if the Great Mercy Pope of beloved memory anticipated projects like Vinny Flynn's book that would make the case for the *Diary*. Notice especially how he refers to St. Faustina's *Diary* "as a particular Gospel of Divine Mercy, written from a twentieth-century perspective" and then highlights "Christ, crucified and risen, just as he appeared to Sister Faustina" as the "supreme revelation" of the truth that God, who is Love, can always draw good from evil:

> I have chosen here to speak of Sister Faustina and the devotion to the merciful Christ which she promoted, because she too belongs to our time. She lived in the first decades of the twentieth century and died before the Second World War. In that very period the mystery of Divine Mercy was revealed to her, and what she experienced she then recorded in her *Diary*. To those who survived the Second World War, Saint Faustina's *Diary* appears as a particular Gospel of Divine Mercy, written from a twentieth-century perspective. The people of that time understood her message. They understood it in the light of the dramatic buildup of evil during the Second World War and the cruelty of the totalitarian systems. It was as if Christ had wanted to reveal that

the limit imposed upon evil, of which man is both perpetrator and victim, is ultimately Divine Mercy. ... God can always draw good from evil, he wills that all should be saved and come to knowledge of the truth (cf. 1 Tim 2:4): God is Love (cf. 1 Jn 4:8). Christ, crucified and risen, just as he appeared to Sister Faustina, is the supreme revelation of this truth (*Memory and Identity: Conversations at the Dawn of a Millennium*, New York: Rizzoli, 2005, pp. 54-55).

Read this excerpt from John Paul's last book again, this time slowly. Ponder its meaning. After you've used this book for prayer and reflection, come back and read these words yet again. You should then have a deeper appreciation of St. Faustina's *Diary* as "a particular Gospel of Divine Mercy" for your own spiritual life.

HOW TO USE THIS BOOK

Ideally, *Mercy's Gaze* is intended for daily prayer and reflection, using one reading each day over the course of 100 days. While you could start it on any day, an opportune time to use it would be over the 40 days of Lent and the 50 days of the Easter season. Given the Divine Mercy focus of the book's readings, it would provide excellent preparation for Divine Mercy Sunday in particular, which is celebrated on the Second Sunday of Easter.

An Orientation. But before you get started, please read the Introduction carefully and slowly. It's packed with meaning and provides a spiritual orientation for approaching the readings. Also, remember that in each reading, Scripture as the inspired Word of God takes primacy of place. It provides the foundation for your time of prayer and reflection. That's why the *Diary* excerpt always appears before the Scripture passage in the readings — to present the *Diary* in the context of Scripture.

Gaze. Begin and end each time of daily prayer and reflection by gazing upon the crucified and risen Lord Jesus in the Divine Mercy Image, which is provided on the inside back cover of this book. Follow Vinny's advice in the Introduction on double gazing: Gaze upon Jesus and receive His gaze. Ask Jesus to transform you into a living image of mercy.

Ponder. After you have read the passages for the day prayerfully and slowly, give yourself enough time to ponder their meaning for your life. Perhaps a word or phrase in one of the passages seems intended for you. Maybe the Lord is helping you understand an aspect of His mercy in a deeper way. Stay with it.

Head knowledge alone isn't enough. Ask Our Lady to help you move from your head to your heart in seeking to understand and apply God's Word. Saint Luke tells us that Mary pondered and reflected in her *heart* as God acted in her life (see Lk 2:19; 2:51).

If you are familiar with *lectio divina* (Latin for divine reading) and have enough time for it, it would be an ideal way to use this book. *Lectio divina* is a traditional Benedictine practice of scriptural reading, meditation, and prayer intended to promote communion with God and to increase one's knowledge of God's Word. It doesn't treat Scripture as simply texts to be studied but as the living Word. During his papacy, Pope Benedict XVI spoke frequently of *lectio divina* and highly recommended it.

My Reflections on the Theme. When you come to the end of the readings for a particular theme, record your thoughts and reflections on the one or two blank pages marked "My Reflections on the Theme." Or record a thought or reflection on these pages every day as you follow the theme.

The Appendix. There is an appendix of mercy prayers drawn from Scripture and the Diary. You may want to use these texts for an extended time of prayer or reflection. After completing the 100 days of reading, you could even draw from them to create more daily readings on mercy.

Note to the Reader. Quotations from the *Diary of St. Maria Faustina Kowalska: Divine Mercy in My Soul* are presented here in the style of the English edition. Thus, the words of the Lord to Faustina are in bold, and those of Our Lady are in italics. The numbers set off by dashes or in parentheses represent the corresponding paragraph numbers in the *Diary*.

My prayer is that, as you read *Mercy's Gaze*, you will grow in your appreciation for God's awe-inspiring revelations of Divine Mercy, both in Sacred Scripture and in the *Diary*. God's mercy is truly the heart of the Gospel, and it is *the* message for our times. What a gift Jesus has given us in Divine Mercy to guide us home to the House of the Father! And on our way home, let's keep gazing at Jesus, pondering His message, and trusting in Him.

— David C. Came
Executive Editor of Marian Press

INTRODUCTION

"O Eternal Love, You command Your
Sacred Image to be painted" (*Diary*, 1).

So begins the *Diary of St. Faustina*, written by a simple,
uneducated Polish nun, who was destined to become the first saint
of the Jubilee Year that ushered in the third Christian millennium.

It seems fitting that her *Diary* should begin this way, for
the painting of Christ as He appeared to her — known now
throughout the world as the Divine Mercy Image — reveals to
those who look deeply the entire message of mercy that comes
from the 600-page *Diary*.

Why did the Lord appear to her and command that this
image be painted? The clue comes in an easily overlooked phrase
in Faustina's dramatic description of this first major revelation
recorded in the *Diary*. The Lord has just appeared to her, dressed
in the white robe of the priesthood, with His right hand raised
in blessing and His left hand holding His garment open in the
area of His Heart, from which gush forth red and pale rays as
an endless fountain of mercy. Faustina writes: "I kept my gaze
fixed on the Lord" (*Diary*, 47).

Filled with "awe, but also with great joy," Faustina says
nothing, but simply keeps her gaze fixed on Christ. The Lord
doesn't immediately speak to her either, but only "after a while"
tells her to paint His image. He first gives her time to contemplate
in her mind and heart what she is seeing with her eyes — to look
as Our Lady looked, pondering in her heart deeply so that she
could enter more fully into the mystery of Christ's love, in
complete trust and surrender to His will.

Pope John Paul II (now blessed), who referred to St. Faustina as "a sign for our times," considered this type of contemplative gazing so important that he proclaimed it as the agenda of the Church for the next thousand years. "To contemplate the face of Jesus," he wrote in his encyclical on the Eucharist, "and to contemplate it with Mary, is the 'programme' which I have set before the Church at the dawn of the third millennium" (*Ecclesia de Eucharistia*, 6).

The *Catechism of the Catholic Church* also stresses the importance of this gazing upon the Lord, connecting it with the daily conversion we all need. "The human heart," it tells us, "is converted by looking upon him whom our sins have pierced" (1432).

How can looking at Jesus convert our hearts? Because when we *really* look, we also see the Father and come to understand His plan of mercy for all.

Jesus is the "image of the invisible God," writes St. Paul (Col 1:15). Who's the "invisible God"? The Father. Jesus Himself makes this clear when He explains to the apostles, "He who has seen me has seen the Father" (Jn 14:9).

According to Pope John Paul II, this is why Jesus came — to show us that God is a Father who is "rich in mercy. ... Believing in the crucified Son means 'seeing the Father'" (*Dives in Misericordia*, 1, 7).

What's all this have to do with converting our hearts?

"Conversion to God," John Paul continues, "always consists in discovering His mercy, ... [and] is always the fruit of the 'rediscovery' of this Father, who is rich in mercy" (*Dives in Misericordia*, 13).

So, when we gaze upon Christ as He is represented in this image — not only with our eyes but with our minds and hearts — we "rediscover" the Father. We recognize that it's *His* hand raised over us in blessing, *His* mercy gushing forth from the Heart of Jesus. We come to know who Christ is, who the Father is, and who we are called to be, and we are progressively transformed into living images of mercy.

Christ didn't command this image to be painted so that we could simply hang it on a wall and glance at it now and then. We are not supposed to just *look* at this image; we are supposed to become it.

As St. Paul explains, "All of us, gazing with unveiled faces upon the glory of the Lord, are being transformed into the same image from glory to glory" (2 Cor 3:18).

Saint Faustina's spiritual director, Blessed Fr. Michael Sopocko, in recounting her instructions for the painting of the image, emphasizes that it should be painted in such a way that our gazing upon it also reveals to us the compassionate gaze of Jesus.

Cardinal Joseph Ratzinger (now Pope Emeritus Benedict XVI) also speaks of this gaze of Christ, explaining that communicating with Christ demands not only that we gaze on Him but also that we "allow him to gaze on us, listen to him, get to know him" (*God Is Near Us*, San Francisco: Ignatius Press, 2003, p. 97).

This gazing upon Christ — and receiving His gaze — changes us, transforms us, bit-by-bit, healing our hearts and enabling us to entrust our lives to Him. It is this double gazing that I invite you to experience as you read this book. Don't attempt to consume it quickly, all at once, but sit for a while with each entry. Ponder it to make it your own and allow it to touch your life. Take the time to contemplate the face of Jesus. Get to know Him and listen in your heart to what He wants to say to you today through Sacred Scripture and the *Diary of St. Faustina*.

Looking upon Jesus in this way and seeing how He looks at you with love, may you come to recognize and embrace the mystery of the Father's mercy — the love that is greater than all sin, greater than all evil; the love that can reach the darkest corners of the world and heal all our brokenness; the love that we don't deserve and can't earn, but that is freely given; the love that can fill us to overflowing, transforming us, like St. Faustina, into living images of mercy for others.

— Vinny Flynn

The DIVINE MERCY MESSAGE *and* DEVOTION

Illumined by Sacred Scripture, here are four key elements of the message and devotion that Jesus gave to St. Faustina for our time: the Divine Mercy Image, the Chaplet of Divine Mercy, the Three O'clock Hour, and Divine Mercy Sunday (the "Feast of Mercy") Notice how they invariably point to the Passion, death, and Resurrection of Jesus Christ. The Paschal mystery is the source of their amazing power to transform our lives.

For as we gaze on the Lord in the Divine Mercy Image, pray the Chaplet of Divine Mercy for souls, remember the Lord's death at the Three O'clock Hour, and celebrate Divine Mercy Sunday each year, we enter more deeply into the timeless reality of what our Merciful Savior accomplished on the Cross out of love for us.

The
DIVINE MERCY
IMAGE

1. The Great High Priest

I saw the Lord Jesus clothed in a white garment. One hand [was] raised in the gesture of blessing, the other was touching the garment at the breast. From beneath the garment, slightly drawn aside at the breast, there were emanating two large rays, one red, the other pale.

— Diary, 47

I saw one like the Son of Man, clothed with a long robe. ... The brightness was like the sun; rays came forth from his hand, where his power lay hidden.

— Revelation 1:13; Habakkuk 3:4

2. Gazing on the Lord

In silence I kept my gaze fixed on the Lord; my soul was struck with awe, but also with great joy. After a while, Jesus said to me, **Paint an image according to the pattern you see, with the signature: Jesus, I trust in You. I desire that this image be venerated, first in your chapel, and [then] throughout the world. ... I promise that the soul that will venerate this image will not perish. I also promise victory over [its] enemies already here on earth, especially at the hour of death. I Myself will defend it as My own glory.**

— Diary, 47, 48

He is the image of the invisible God, the firstborn of all creation. ... the reflection of God's glory and the exact imprint of God's very being. ... All of us, gazing with unveiled face on the glory of the Lord, are being transformed into the same image from glory to glory.

— Colossians 1:15; Hebrews 1:3; 2 Corinthians 3:18 (NAB)

3. 'Blood and Water'

During prayer I heard these words within me: **The two rays denote Blood and Water. The pale ray stands for the Water which makes souls righteous. The red ray stands for the Blood which is the life of souls. ... These two rays issued forth from the very depths of My tender mercy when My agonized Heart was opened by a lance on the Cross. These rays shield souls from the wrath of My Father. Happy is the one who will dwell in their shelter, for the just hand of God shall not lay hold of him.**

— Diary, 299

This is the one who came by water and blood, Jesus Christ, not with the water only but with the water and the blood. And the Spirit is the one that testifies, for the Spirit is the truth. There are three that testify: the Spirit and the water and the blood, and these three agree. ... And this is the testimony: God gave us eternal life, and this life is in his Son. Whoever has the Son has life; whoever does not have the Son of God does not have life.

— 1 John 5:6-8, 11-12

4. Rays of Mercy

This day I take into my hands the two rays that spring from Your merciful Heart; that is, the Blood and the Water; and I scatter them all over the globe so that each soul may receive Your mercy and, having received it, may glorify it for endless ages.

— Diary, 836

When they came to Jesus and saw that he was already dead, they did not break his legs. Instead, one of the soldiers pierced his side with a spear, and at once blood and water came out.

— John 19:33-34

The CHAPLET of
DIVINE MERCY

5. A Powerful Prayer of Atonement

I saw an Angel ... about to strike the earth. ... I found myself pleading with God for the world with words heard interiorly. As I was praying in this manner, I saw the Angel's helplessness; he could not carry out the just punishment which was rightly due for sins. ... The words with which I entreated God are these: **Eternal Father, I offer You the Body and Blood, Soul and Divinity of Your dearly beloved Son, Our Lord Jesus Christ for our sins and those of the whole world, for the sake of His sorrowful Passion, have mercy on us.**

— Diary, 474-475

For God so loved the world that he gave his only Son, so that everyone who believes in him may not perish but may have eternal life. ... He had to become like his brothers and sisters in every respect, so that he might be a merciful and faithful high priest in the service of God. ... He is the atoning sacrifice for our sins, and not for ours only but also for the sins of the whole world.

— John 3:16; Hebrews 2:17; 1 John 2:2

6. Calming the Storm

Today I was awakened by a great storm. ... I began to pray that the storm would do no harm, when I heard the words: **Say the chaplet I have taught you, and the storm will cease.** I began immediately to say the chaplet and hadn't even finished it when the storm suddenly ceased, and I heard the words: **Through the chaplet you will obtain everything, if what you ask for is compatible with My will.**

— Diary, 1731

A windstorm arose on the sea, so great that the boat was being swamped by the waves; but he was asleep. And they went and woke him up, saying, "Lord, save us! We are perishing!" And he said to them, "Why are you afraid, you of little faith?" Then he got up and rebuked the winds and the sea; and there was a dead calm.

— Matthew 8:24-26

The HOUR of
GREAT MERCY

7. Prayer at Three O'clock

At three o'clock, implore My mercy, especially for sinners; and, if only for a brief moment, immerse yourself in My Passion, particularly in My abandonment at the moment of agony. This is the hour of great mercy for the whole world. ... In this hour, I will refuse nothing to the soul that makes a request of Me in virtue of My Passion. ... In this hour you can obtain everything for yourself and for others for the asking; it was the hour of grace for the whole world — mercy triumphed over justice.

— *Diary*, 1320, 1572

When it was noon, darkness came over the whole land until three in the afternoon. At three o'clock Jesus cried out with a loud voice, "Eloi, Eloi, lema sabachthani?" which means, "My God, my God, why have you forsaken me?"

— Mark 15:33-34

The FEAST of
MERCY

8. Floodgates of Mercy

I desire that there be a Feast of Mercy. I want this image, which you will paint with a brush, to be solemnly blessed on the first Sunday after Easter; that Sunday is to be the Feast of Mercy. ... I desire that the Feast of Mercy be a refuge and shelter for all souls, and especially for poor sinners. On that day the very depths of My tender mercy are open. I pour out a whole ocean of graces upon those souls who approach the fount of My mercy. ... On that day all the divine floodgates through which grace flow are opened.

— Diary, 49, 699

On the last and greatest day of the feast, Jesus stood up and exclaimed, "Let anyone who thirsts come to me and drink. Whoever believes in me, as scripture says: 'Rivers of living water will flow from within him.'" ... On that day, the mountains shall drip new wine, and the hills shall flow with milk, All the streams of Judah will flow with water. A spring will rise from the house of the Lord, watering the Valley

— John 7:37-38 (NAB); Joel 4:18 (NAB)

My Reflections
on the Theme

My Reflections
on the Theme

ABC'S *of* Mercy

Remember how your parents and teachers drilled you in your ABC's as a foundation for learning to read? You had to learn your letters by heart before sounding them out in actual words.

Well, now it's time to learn by heart the ABC's of Mercy, so Divine Mercy as a way of life becomes second nature in every situation you encounter. The letter "A" stands for "Ask for His mercy." "B" is for "Be merciful to others." "C" stands for "Completely trust in Jesus." Keep it up. Keep repeating it. Keep living it.

ASK *for* MERCY

9. The Door of Mercy

Souls that make an appeal to My mercy delight Me. To such souls I grant even more graces than they ask. I cannot punish even the greatest sinner if he makes an appeal to My compassion, but on the contrary, I justify him in My unfathomable and inscrutable mercy. ... Before I come as a just Judge, I first open wide the door of My mercy. He who refuses to pass through the door of My mercy must pass through the door of My justice.

— *Diary*, 1146

"Ask and you will receive; seek and you will find; knock, and the door will be opened to you. For everyone who asks, receives; and the one who seeks, finds; and to the one who knocks, the door will be opened."

— Luke 11:9-10 (NAB)

B
BE MERCIFUL

10. The Demands of Mercy

Yes, the first Sunday after Easter is the Feast of Mercy, but there must also be acts of mercy, and I demand the worship of My mercy through the solemn celebration of the Feast and through the veneration of the image which is painted. By means of this image I shall grant many graces to souls. It is to be a reminder of the demands of My mercy, because even the strongest faith is of no avail without works.

— Diary, 742

What good is it, my brothers and sisters, if you say you have faith but do not have works? ... For just as the body without the spirit is dead, so faith without works is also dead.

— James 2:14, 26

11. Judged by Mercy

There are three ways of performing an act of mercy: the merciful word, by forgiving and by comforting; secondly, if you can offer no word, then pray — that too is mercy; and thirdly, deeds of mercy. And when the Last Day comes, we shall be judged from this, and on this basis we shall receive the eternal verdict.

— Diary, 1158

Then the king will say to those on his right, "Come, you who are blessed by my Father. Inherit the kingdom prepared for you from the foundation of the world. For I was hungry and you gave me food, I was thirsty and you gave me drink, a stranger and you welcomed me, naked and you clothed me, ill and you cared for me, in prison and you visited me. ... Amen, I say to you, whatever you did for one of these least brothers of mine, you did for me."

— Matthew 25:34-36, 40 (NAB)

12. Reflecting the Father's Love

The Lord said to me, **It should be of no concern to you how anyone else acts; you are to be My living reflection, through love and mercy.** I answered, "Lord, but they often take advantage of my goodness." **That makes no difference, My daughter. That is no concern of yours. As for you, be always merciful toward other people, and especially toward sinners.**

— *Diary*, 1446

Do not repay evil for evil or abuse for abuse; but, on the contrary, repay with a blessing. ... "If you love those who love you, what credit is that to you? For even sinners love those who love them. If you do good to those who do good to you, what credit is that to you? For even sinners do the same." ... "But love your enemies, do good, and lend, expecting nothing in return." ... "Be merciful, just as your Father is merciful."

— 1 Peter 3:9; Luke 6:32-33, 35, 36

13. We Kill with the Tongue

When I receive Jesus in Holy Communion, I ask Him fervently to deign to heal my tongue so that I would offend neither God nor neighbor by it. ... Great are the faults committed by the tongue. ... The tongue is a small member, but it does big things. ... I tremble to think that I have to give an account of my tongue. ... Help me, O Lord, that my tongue may be merciful, so that I should never speak negatively of my neighbor, but have a word of comfort and forgiveness for all.

— *Diary*, 92, 118-119, 163

The tongue is a small member, yet it boasts of great exploits. How great a forest is set ablaze by a small fire! And the tongue is a fire. ... With it we bless the Lord and Father, and with it we curse those who are made in the likeness of God. From the same mouth come blessing and cursing. ... "I tell you, on the day of judgment you will have to give an account for every careless word you utter; for by your words you will be justified, and by your words you will be condemned."

— James 3:5-6, 9-10; Matthew 12:36-37

C
COMPLETELY TRUST

14. Vessel of Grace

I am offering people a vessel with which they are to keep coming for graces to the fountain of mercy. That vessel is this image with the signature: "Jesus, I trust in You." ... The graces of My mercy are drawn by means of one vessel only, and that is — trust. The more a soul trusts, the more it will receive. Souls that trust boundlessly are a great comfort to Me, because I pour all the treasures of My graces into them.

— *Diary*, 327, 1578

Blessed are those who trust in the Lord, whose trust is the Lord. They shall be like a tree planted by water, sending out its roots by the stream. It shall not fear when heat comes, and its leaves shall stay green. ... O Lord of hosts, happy is everyone who trusts in you.

— Jeremiah 17:7-8; Psalm 84:12

15. Trusting against All Hope

I understand souls who are suffering against hope, for I have gone through that fire myself. But God will not give [us anything] beyond our strength. Often have I lived hoping against hope, and have advanced my hope to complete trust in God. Let that which He has ordained from all ages happen to me.

— *Diary*, 386

Abraham believed God, and it was reckoned to him as righteousness. ... Hoping against hope, he believed. ... No distrust made him waver concerning the promise of God, but he grew strong in his faith as he gave glory to God, being fully convinced that God was able to do what he had promised.

— Romans 4:3, 18, 20-21

16. No Fear

Although the path is very thorny, I do not fear to go ahead. Even if a hailstorm of persecutions covers me; even if my friends forsake me, even if all things conspire against me, and the horizon grows dark; even if a raging storm breaks out, and I feel I am quite alone and must brave it all; still, fully at peace, I will trust in Your mercy, O my God.

— Diary, 1195

This extraordinary power belongs to God and does not come from us. We are afflicted in every way, but not crushed; perplexed, but not driven to despair; persecuted, but not forsaken; struck down, but not destroyed. ... Even though I walk through the darkest valley, I fear no evil; for you are with me; your rod and your staff — they comfort me.

— 2 Corinthians 4:7-9; Psalm 23:4

17. Don't Act on Your Own

I have come to know that, in order for God to act in a soul, it must give up acting on its own; otherwise, God will not carry out His will in it.

— Diary, 1790

Commit your way to the Lord; trust in him, and he will act.

— Psalm 37:5

My Reflections
on the Theme

My Reflections
on the Theme

The EUCHARIST
and THANKSGIVING

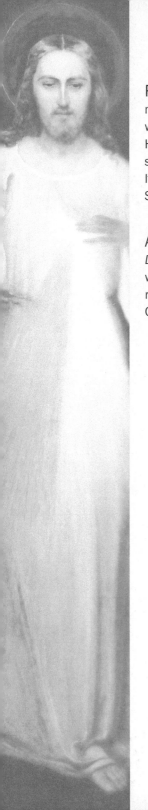

Receiving Jesus daily in Holy Communion meant everything to St. Faustina. Her Eucharistic Lord was the source of her strength as she faced life's trials. Her union with Him was her comfort and joy — a sweet foretaste of being with Him forever in heaven. It's no surprise, then, that her full religious name was Sr. Maria Faustina of the Most Blessed Sacrament.

As you read the following Scripture and *Diary* passages, consider Jesus in the Eucharist and who He is for you. Do you prepare your heart to receive Him in Holy Communion? After receiving Communion, do you thank Jesus for His presence?

The
EUCHARIST

18. 'Prisoner of Love'

O King of Glory, though You hide Your beauty, yet the eye of my soul rends the veil. I see the angelic choirs giving You honor without cease, and all the heavenly Powers praising You without cease, and without cease they are saying: Holy, Holy, Holy. Oh, who will comprehend Your love and Your unfathomable mercy toward us! O Prisoner of Love, I lock up my poor heart in this tabernacle, that it may adore You without cease night and day.

— *Diary*, 80

I saw the Lord sitting on a throne. ... Seraphs were in attendance above him. ... And one called to another and said: "Holy, holy, holy is the Lord of hosts; the whole earth is full of his glory." ... Day and night without ceasing they sing, "Holy, holy, holy, the Lord God the Almighty, who was and is and is to come."

— Isaiah 6:1-3; Revelation 4:8

19. One Thing Sustains Me

I find myself so weak that were it not for Holy Communion I would fall continually. One thing alone sustains me, and that is Holy Communion. From it I draw my strength; in it is all my comfort. I fear life on days when I do not receive Holy Communion. I fear my own self. Jesus concealed in the Host is everything to me. From the tabernacle I draw strength, power, courage, and light. Here, I seek consolation in time of anguish.

— *Diary*, 1037

O God, you are my God — for you I long! For you my body yearns; for you my soul thirsts, like a land parched, lifeless, and without water. So I look to you in the sanctuary to see your power and glory. For your love is better than life; my lips offer you worship! I will bless you as long as I live; I will lift up my hands, calling on your name.

— Psalm 63:1-5 (NAB)

20. Living Eucharist

I often feel God's presence after Holy Communion in a special and tangible way. I know God is in my heart. And the fact that I feel Him in my heart does not interfere with my duties. Even when I am dealing with very important matters which require attention, I do not lose the presence of God in my soul, and I am closely united with Him. With Him I go to work, with Him I go for recreation, with Him I suffer, with Him I rejoice; I live in Him and He in me. I am never alone, because He is my constant companion. He is present to me at every moment.

— *Diary*, 318

"Those who eat my flesh and drink my blood abide in me, and I in them." ... I have been crucified with Christ; and it is no longer I who live, but it is Christ who lives in me. And the life I now live in the flesh I live by faith in the Son of God, who loved me and gave himself for me.

— John 6:56: Galatians 2:19-20

21. Dwelling Place for the Trinity

Once after Holy Communion, I heard these words: You are Our dwelling place. At that moment, I felt in my soul the presence of the Holy Trinity, the Father, the Son and the Holy Spirit. ... My soul is in communion with these Three; but I do not know how to express this in words; yet my soul understands it well. Whoever is united to One of the Three Persons is thereby united to the whole Blessed Trinity, for this Oneness is indivisible.

— *Diary*, 451, 472

"Those who love me will keep my word, and my Father will love them, and we will come to them and make our home with them." ... "And I will ask the Father, and he will give you another Advocate, ... the Spirit of truth. ... You know him, because he abides with you, and he will be in you."

— John 14:23, 16-17

22. Dissolving in God

O Jesus! I sense keenly how Your divine Blood is circulating in my heart; I have not the least doubt that Your most pure love has entered my heart with Your most sacred Blood. I am aware that You are dwelling in me, together with the Father and the Holy Spirit, or rather I am aware that it is I who am living in You, O incomprehensible God! I am aware that I am dissolving in You like a drop in an ocean. I am aware that You are within me and all about me, that You are in all things that surround me, in all that happens to me.

— Diary, 478

"I am in my Father, and you in me, and I in you."

— John 14:20

23. Receiving Unworthily

Today, the Lord told me, **My daughter, write that it pains Me very much when religious souls receive the Sacrament of Love merely out of habit, as if they did not distinguish this food. I find neither faith nor love in their hearts. I go to such souls with great reluctance. It would be better if they did not receive Me.**

— Diary, 1288

Whoever, therefore, eats the bread or drinks the cup of the Lord in an unworthy manner will be answerable for the body and blood of the Lord. Examine yourselves, and only then eat of the bread and drink of the cup. For all who eat and drink without discerning the body, eat and drink judgment against themselves.

— 1 Corinthians 11:27-29

24. One Hour at the Altar

One hour spent at the foot of the altar in the greatest dryness of spirit is dearer to me than a hundred years of worldly pleasures.

— *Diary*, 254

How lovely is your dwelling place, O Lord of hosts! ... For a day in your courts is better than a thousand elsewhere.

— Psalm 84:1, 10

25. 'Eternal Life'

I want to tell you that eternal life must begin already, here on earth through Holy Communion. Each Holy Communion makes you more capable of communing with God throughout eternity.

— *Diary*, 1811

"Father, ... this is eternal life, that they may know you, the only true God, and Jesus Christ whom you have sent." ... "Those who eat my flesh and drink my blood have eternal life."

— John 17:1, 3; John 6:54

26. A Child's Eucharist

Hidden Jesus, in You lies all my strength. From my most tender years, the Lord Jesus in the Blessed Sacrament has attracted me to Himself. ... When I was seven years old, at a Vesper Service, conducted before the Lord Jesus in the monstrance, the love of God was imparted to me for the first time and filled my little heart; and the Lord gave me understanding of divine things. From that day until this, my love for the hidden God has been growing constantly to the point of closest intimacy. All the strength of my soul flows from the Blessed Sacrament. I spend all my free moments in conversation with Him.

— Diary, 1404

At that time Jesus said, "I thank you, Father, Lord of heaven and earth, because you have hidden these things from the wise and the intelligent and have revealed them to infants; yes, Father, for such was your gracious will."

— Matthew 11:25-26

THANKSGIVING

27. All Is Gift

In You, O Lord, all is good, all is a gift of Your paternal Heart. I do not prefer consolations over bitterness or bitterness over consolations, but thank You, O Jesus, for everything!

— Diary, 343

Let the peace of Christ rule in your hearts. And be thankful. ... Give thanks in all circumstances; for this is the will of God in Christ Jesus for you.

— Colossians 3:15; 1 Thessalonians 5:18

My Reflections
on the Theme

My Reflections
on the Theme

CONFESSION
and FORGIVENESS

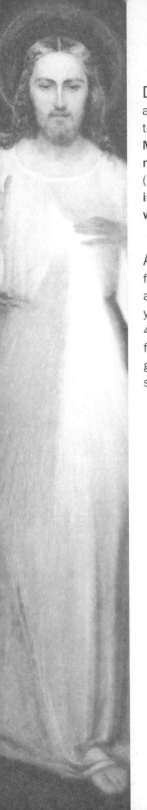

Do you want to receive spiritual healing and restoration as a child of God? Then, as Jesus tells St. Faustina, come often to **"the Tribunal of Mercy** [the Sacrament of Reconciliation]" where **"the miracle of Divine Mercy restores** [the] **soul in full"** (*Diary*, 1448). And when you come, **"open your soul in confession as you would to Me, and I will fill it with My light"** (*Diary*, 1725).

As you experience God's healing and forgiveness, discover that there is no limit to His mercy and that you resemble Him most when you forgive your neighbor, "as God in Christ has forgiven you" (Eph 4:32). Recall the leper who returned to thank Jesus for his healing (see Lk 17:11-19). Express your own gratitude to God for healing you from "the leprosy of sin" through the Sacrament of Confession.

CONFESSION

28. We Come to Be Healed

Today I heard the words: ... **I do not want to punish aching mankind, but I desire to heal it, pressing it to My Merciful Heart**. ... We come to confession to be healed. ... When I leave the confessional, I shall rouse in my soul great gratitude to the Holy Trinity for this wonderful and inconceivable miracle of mercy that is wrought in my soul.

— *Diary*, 1588, 377, 225

Therefore confess your sins ... so that you may be healed. ... And as he entered a village, he was met by ten lepers, who stood at a distance and lifted up their voices and said, "Jesus, Master, have mercy on us." When he saw them he said, "Go and show yourselves to the priests." And as they went they were cleansed. Then one of them, when he saw that he was healed, turned back, praising God with a loud voice; and he fell on his face at Jesus' feet, giving him thanks.

— James 5:16; Luke 17:12-16

29. 'Tribunal of Mercy'

Tell souls where they are to look for solace; that is, in the Tribunal of Mercy [the Sacrament of Reconciliation]. **There the greatest miracles take place. ... It suffices to come with faith to the feet of My representative and to reveal to him one's misery, and the miracle of Divine Mercy will be fully demonstrated. Were a soul like a decaying corpse so that from a human standpoint, there would be no** [hope of] **restoration and everything would already be lost, it is not so with God. The miracle of Divine Mercy restores that soul in full.**

— *Diary*, 1448

"Which is easier, to say to the paralytic, 'Your sins are forgiven,' or to say, 'Rise, pick up your mat and walk?' But that you may know that the Son of Man has authority to forgive sins on earth" — he said to the paralytic, "I say to you, rise, pick up your mat and go home." He rose, picked up his mat at once, and went away in the sight of everyone.

— Mark 2:9-12 (NAB)

30. Priest Only a Screen

Today the Lord said to me, ... **When you approach the confessional, know this, that I Myself am waiting there for you. I am only hidden by the priest, but I Myself act in your soul. Here the misery of the soul meets the God of mercy. ... You make your confession before Me. The person of the priest is, for Me, only a screen. Never analyze what sort of a priest it is that I am making use of; open your soul in confession as you would to Me, and I will fill it with My light.**

— *Diary*, 1602, 1725

"As the Father has sent me, so I send you." When he had said this, he breathed on them and said to them, "Receive the Holy Spirit. If you forgive the sins of any, they are forgiven them; if you retain the sins of any, they are retained." ... "Truly I tell you, whatever you bind on earth will be bound in heaven, and whatever you loose on earth will be loosed in heaven."

— John 20:21-23; Matthew 18:18

FORGIVENESS

31. No Limit

To me who am so miserable, You have shown Your mercy, O God, and this, time and time again. You carry me in the bosom of Your mercy and forgive me every time that I ask Your forgiveness with a contrite heart. … **You are dealing with the God of mercy, which your misery cannot exhaust. Remember, I did not allot only a certain number of pardons. … Do not lose heart in coming for pardon, for I am always ready to forgive you. … As often as you come to Me, humbling yourself and asking My forgiveness, I pour out a superabundance of graces on your soul, and your imperfection vanishes before My eyes, and I see only your love and your humility.**

— Diary, 1332, 1488, 1293

The Lord is merciful and gracious, slow to anger and abounding in steadfast love. He will not always accuse, nor will he keep his anger forever. He does not deal with us according to our sins, nor repay us according to our iniquities. … Seek the Lord while he may be found, call upon him while he is near; let the wicked forsake their way, and the unrighteous their thoughts; let them return to the Lord, that he may have mercy on them, and to our God, for he will abundantly pardon.

— Psalm 103:8-10; Isaiah 55:6-7

32. Resembling God

We resemble God most when we forgive our neighbors. God is Love, Goodness, and Mercy.

— Diary, 1148

Put away from you all bitterness and wrath and anger and wrangling and slander, together with all malice, and be kind to one another, tenderhearted, forgiving one another, as God in Christ has forgiven you.

— Ephesians 4:31-32

My Reflections
on the Theme

My Reflections
on the Theme

The WILL of GOD

Most of us struggle to discern God's will for our lives. It ranges from seeking to do God's will every day to discerning His will for our vocation and state of life. Am I called to the married life, or should I consider the priesthood or the religious life? If I'm married with children and have a good career, what else is God calling me to do?

In these passages, learn how discerning God's will starts with our desire to please and serve Him above all else. As St. Faustina writes, "I always consider what is most pleasing to Jesus" (*Diary*, 380).

The WILL of GOD

33. Lips to the Cup

I thank You, Jesus, You who first drank the cup of bitterness before You gave it to me, in a much milder form. I put my lips to this cup of Your holy will. Let all be done according to Your good pleasure. … I want to drink the cup to its last drop, and not seek to know the reason why.

— *Diary*, 343

Jesus said to them, … "Are you able to drink the cup that I drink, or be baptized with the baptism that I am baptized with?" They replied, "We are able." Then Jesus said to them, "The cup that I drink you will drink; and with the baptism with which I am baptized, you will be baptized."

— Mark 10:38-39

34. Nothing by Chance

May You be blessed, O God, for everything You send me. Nothing under the sun happens without Your will.

— *Diary*, 1208

"Are not two sparrows sold for a small coin? Yet not one of them falls to the ground without your Father's knowledge. Even all the hairs of your head are counted. So do not be afraid; you are worth more than many sparrows."

— Matthew 10:29-31 (NAB)

35. Pleasing God

I make no movement, no gesture after my own liking, because I am bound by grace; I always consider what is more pleasing to Jesus.

— Diary, 380

"I do nothing on my own, but I speak these things as the Father instructed me. And the one who sent me is with me; he has not left me alone, for I always do what is pleasing to him."

— John 8:28-29

36. Happiness

Before All Souls' Day, I went to the cemetery at dusk. Although it was locked, I managed to open the gate a bit and said, "If you need something, my dear little souls, I will be glad to help you to the extent that the rule permits me." I then heard these words, "Do the will of God; we are happy in the measure that we have fulfilled God's will."

— Diary, 518

Happy are those whose way is blameless, who walk in the law of the Lord. Happy are those who keep his decrees, who seek him with their whole heart, who also do no wrong, but walk in his ways.

— Psalm 119:1-3

37. 'My Daily Food'

There is one word I heed and continually ponder; it alone is everything to me; I live by it and die by it, and it is the holy will of God. It is my daily food. My whole soul listens intently to God's wishes. I do always what God asks of me, although my nature often quakes and I feel that the magnitude of these things is beyond my strength. ... From today onward, Your will, Lord, is my food. Take my whole being; dispose of me as You please. Whatever Your fatherly hand gives me, I will accept with submission, peace and joy. ... helped by Your grace I will carry out everything You demand of me.

— Diary, 652, 1264

The disciples were urging him, "Rabbi, eat something." But he said to them, "I have food to eat that you do not know about." ... "My food is to do the will of him who sent me and to complete his work." ... "I have come down from heaven, not to do my own will, but the will of him who sent me."

— John 4:31-32, 34; 6:38

38. 'A Great Offense'

I understood that all striving for perfection and all sanctity consist in doing God's will. Perfect fulfillment of God's will is maturity in sanctity; there is no room for doubt here. To receive God's light and recognize what God wants of us and yet not do it is a great offense against the majesty of God. Such a soul deserves to be completely forsaken by God. It resembles Lucifer, who had great light, but did not do God's will.

— Diary, 666

"Everyone who hears these words of mine and does not act on them will be like a foolish man who built his house on sand. The rain fell, and the floods came, and the winds blew and beat against that house, and it fell — and great was its fall!" ... How much worse punishment do you think will be deserved by those who have spurned the Son of God?

— Matthew 7:26-27; Hebrews 10:29

39. 'Faithful Submission'

Faithful submission to the will of God, always and everywhere, in all events and circumstances of life, gives great glory to God. Such submission to the will of God carries more weight with Him than long fasts, mortifications and the most severe penances. Oh, how great is the reward for one act of loving submission to the will of God!

— Diary, 724

Be doers of the word, and not merely hearers. ... "Not everyone who says to me, 'Lord, Lord,' will enter the kingdom of heaven, but only the one who does the will of my Father in heaven."

— James 1:22; Matthew 7:21

40. The Light of God

The Lord has given me the light to know His will more profoundly and to abandon myself completely to the holy will of God. This light has confirmed me in profound peace, making me understand that I should fear nothing except sin. Whatever God sends me, I accept with complete submission to His holy will. Wherever He puts me, I will try faithfully to do His holy will, as well as His wishes, to the extent of my power to do so.

— Diary, 1394

Your word is a lamp to my feet, and a light to my path. I have sworn an oath and confirmed it, to observe your righteous ordinances. ... "I am the light of the world. Whoever follows me will never walk in darkness but will have the light of life."

— Psalm 119:105-106; John 8:12

41. 'Self-Denial'

Now I understand well that what unites our soul most closely
to God is self-denial; that is, joining our will to the will of God.
This is what makes the soul truly free, contributes to profound
recollection of the spirit, and makes all life's burdens light, and
death sweet.

— Diary, 462

"Take my yoke upon you, and learn from me; for I am gentle and
humble in heart, and you will find rest for your souls. For my yoke
is easy, and my burden is light."

— Matthew 11:29-30

My Reflections
on the Theme

My Reflections
on the Theme

REDEMPTIVE
SUFFERING

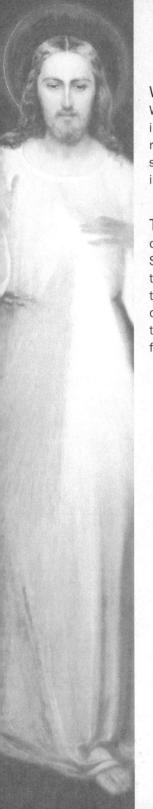

Why we suffer in this life remains a mystery.
We find especially disturbing the suffering of the
innocent. Yet we know that our suffering can have
redemptive value for souls when we unite it to the
suffering of Christ on the Cross — the spotless and
innocent Lamb of God.

The question then becomes: Will we waste
our suffering or use it well for the salvation of souls?
Saint Faustina was quick to unite all her sufferings to
the Lord's and on occasion would even experience
their sweetness. She writes of writhing in terrible pain
on one occasion and of how "my soul came to desire
this sweet agony, which I would not have exchanged
for all the world's treasures" (*Diary*, 1454).

REDEMPTIVE SUFFERING

42. 'The Value of Suffering'

The purer our love becomes, the less there will be within us for the flames of suffering to feed upon, and the suffering will cease to be a suffering for us; it will become a delight! ... Oh, if only the suffering soul knew how it is loved by God, it would die of joy and excess of happiness! Some day, we will know the value of suffering, but then we will no longer be able to suffer. The present moment is ours.

— Diary, 303, 963

I will turn their mourning into joy, I will comfort them, and give them gladness for sorrow. ... Those who go out weeping, bearing the seed for sowing, shall come home with shouts of joy, carrying their sheaves. ... "You have pain now; but I will see you again, and your hearts will rejoice, and no one will take your joy from you."

— Jeremiah 31:13; Psalm 126:6; John 16:22

43. 'The Throne of Grace'

Suffering is a great grace; through suffering the soul becomes like the Savior; in suffering love becomes crystallized; the greater the suffering, the purer the love. ... When I feel that the suffering is more than I can bear, I take refuge in the Lord in the Blessed Sacrament, and I speak to Him with profound silence.

— Diary, 57, 73

Let us therefore approach the throne of grace with boldness, so that we may receive mercy and find grace to help in time of need.

— Hebrews 4:16

44. 'Unimaginable Glory'

The Lord also gave me to understand what unimaginable glory awaits the person who resembles the suffering Jesus here on earth. That person will resemble Jesus in His glory. The Heavenly Father will recognize and glorify our soul to the extent that He sees in us a resemblance to His Son.

— Diary, 604

Rejoice in so far as you are sharing Christ's sufferings, so that you may also be glad and shout for joy when his glory is revealed. ... If, in fact, we suffer with him, ... we may also be glorified with him. I consider that the sufferings of this present time are not worth comparing with the glory about to be revealed to us.

— 1 Peter 4:13; Romans 8:17-18

45. 'Consolation'

Night and suffering. ... I writhed in terrible pain until eleven o'clock. I went in spirit to the Tabernacle and uncovered the ciborium, leaning my head on the rim of the cup, and all my tears flowed silently toward the Heart of Him who alone understands what pain and suffering is. And I experienced the sweetness of this suffering, and my soul came to desire this sweet agony, which I would not have exchanged for all the world's treasures. The Lord gave me strength of spirit and love towards those through whom these sufferings came.

— Diary, 1454

Now may our Lord Jesus Christ himself and God our Father, who loved us and through grace gave us eternal comfort and good hope, comfort your hearts and strengthen them in every good work and word. ... For just as the sufferings of Christ are abundant for us, so also our consolation is abundant through Christ.

— 2 Thessalonians 2:16-17; 2 Corinthians 1:5

My Reflections
on the Theme

LOVE

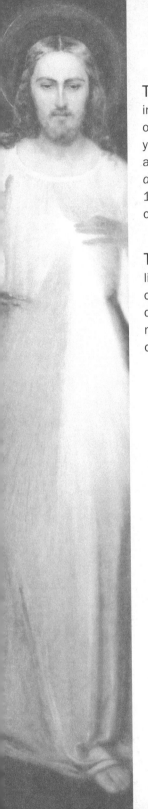

The previous theme could be summed up in the phrase, "Don't waste your suffering." So, too, our present theme could be expressed, "Don't waste your good deeds." For any good deed — even a great act of faith — is worthless in God's eyes if *it is not done out of love*. That's the crystal clear message of 1 Corinthians 13. What matters is our love and not our human effort.

The implication for our busy, success-driven lives is staggering. Instead of just checking off items on our to-do list, we should be checking out the condition of our hearts. As St Faustina puts it, "Nothing, no works, can compare with a single act of pure love of God" (*Diary*, 1092).

LOVE

46. 'Not in Great Deeds'

Jesus, You have given me to know and understand in what a soul's greatness consists: not in great deeds but in great love. Love has its worth, and it confers greatness on all our deeds. Although our actions are small and ordinary in themselves, because of love they become great and powerful before God. ... True greatness is in loving God. ... Only love is of any value; love is greatness; nothing, no works, can compare with a single act of pure love of God.

— Diary, 889, 990, 1092

Love never ends. But as for prophecies, they will come to an end; as for tongues, they will cease; as for knowledge, it will come to an end. ... Faith, hope, and love abide, these three; and the greatest of these is love.

— 1 Corinthians 13:8, 13

47. 'Love Him to Folly'

I have come to understand today that even if I did not accomplish any of the things the Lord is demanding of me, I know that I shall be rewarded as if I had fulfilled everything, because He sees the intention with which I begin, and even if He called me to Himself today, the work would not suffer at all by that, because He Himself is the Lord of both the work and the worker. My part is to love Him to folly; all works are nothing more than a tiny drop before Him. It is love that has meaning and power and merit.

— Diary, 822

If I have all faith, so as to remove mountains, but do not have love, I am nothing. ... "You shall love the Lord your God with all your heart, and with all your soul, and with all your strength, and with all your mind."

— 1 Corinthians 13:2; Luke 10:27

48. Responding to Love

When God loves, He loves with all His Being, with all the power of His Being. If God has loved me in this way, how should I respond — I, His spouse?

— Diary, 392

"As the Father has loved me, so I have loved you; abide in my love. If you keep my commandments, you will abide in my love, just as I have kept my Father's commandments and abide in his love."

— John 15:9-10

49. Nothing Can Separate

I feel that nothing will separate me from the Lord, neither heaven nor earth, neither the present nor the future. ... He, the Immortal Mighty One, makes His will known to me that I may love Him very specially, and He Himself makes my soul capable of the kind of love with which He wants me to love Him. I bury myself more and more in Him, and I fear nothing. ... Nothing can put a stop to my love for You, Jesus, neither suffering, nor adversity, nor fire nor the sword, nor death itself. I feel stronger than all these things. Nothing can compare with love.

— Diary, 947, 340

For I am convinced that neither death, nor life, nor angels, nor rulers, nor things present, nor things to come, nor powers, nor height, nor depth, nor anything else in all creation, will be able to separate us from the love of God in Christ Jesus our Lord.

— Romans 8:38-39

50. Love of Neighbor

O Jesus, I understand that Your mercy is beyond all imagining, and therefore I ask You to make my heart so big that there will be room in it for the needs of all the souls living on the face of the earth. ... O Jesus, make my heart sensitive to all the sufferings of my neighbor, whether of body or of soul.

— Diary, 692

Owe no one anything, except to love one another; for the one who loves another has fulfilled the law. The commandments, "You shall not commit adultery; you shall not murder; you shall not steal; you shall not covet"; and any other commandment, are summed up in this word, "Love your neighbor as yourself." Love does no wrong to a neighbor; therefore, love is the fulfilling of the law.

— Romans 13:8-10

51. Comforting Others

I will always strive to bring assistance, consolation, and all manner of relief to others. My heart is always open to the sufferings of others; and I will not close my heart to the sufferings of others. ... Everyone has a place in my heart and I, in return, have a place in the Heart of Jesus.

— Diary, 871

Blessed be the God and Father of our Lord Jesus Christ, the Father of mercies and the God of all consolation, who consoles us in all our affliction, so that we may be able to console those who are in any affliction with the consolation with which we ourselves are consoled by God.

— 2 Corinthians 1:3-4

52. Love and Fear

Love casts out fear. Since I came to love God with my whole being and with all the strength of my heart, fear has left me. Even if I were to hear the most terrifying things about God's justice, I would not fear Him at all, because I have come to know Him well. God is love, and His Spirit is peace. I see now that my deeds which have flowed from love are more perfect than those which I have done out of fear. I have placed my trust in God and fear nothing. I have given myself over to His holy will; let Him do with me as He wishes, and I will still love Him.

— *Diary*, 589

There is no fear in love, but perfect love casts out fear; for fear has to do with punishment, and whoever fears has not reached perfection in love.

— 1 John 4:18

53. Letter and Spirit

Why are You sad today, Jesus? Tell me, who is the cause of Your sadness? And Jesus answered me, **Chosen souls who do not have My spirit, who live according to the letter and have placed the letter above My spirit, above the spirit of love. I have founded My whole law on love, and yet I do not see love, even in religious orders. This is why sadness fills My Heart.**

— *Diary*, 1478

These people draw near with their mouths and honor me with their lips, while their hearts are far from me, and their worship of me is a human commandment learned by rote. ... "Woe to you, scribes and Pharisees, hypocrites! For you clean the outside of the cup and of the plate, but inside they are full of greed and self-indulgence." ... Our competence is from God, who has made us competent to be ministers of a new covenant, not of letter but of spirit; for the letter kills, but the Spirit gives life.

— Isaiah 29:13; Matthew 23:25; 2 Corinthians 3:5-6

54. 'Lukewarm'

Most Compassionate Jesus, You are Compassion Itself. I bring lukewarm souls into the abode of Your Most Compassionate Heart. In this fire of Your pure love let these tepid souls, who, like corpses, filled You with such deep loathing, be once again set aflame. O Most Compassionate Jesus, exercise the omnipotence of Your mercy and draw them into the very ardor of Your love; and bestow upon them the gift of holy love, for nothing is beyond Your power.

— *Diary,* 1229

"I know your works; you are neither cold nor hot. I wish that you were either cold or hot. So, because you are lukewarm, and neither cold nor hot, I am about to spit you out of my mouth."

— Revelation 3:15-16

My Reflections
on the Theme

My Reflections
on the Theme

STRENGTH
and WEAKNESS

Paradoxes — seeming contradictions to the Christian life — show us that the values of God's kingdom don't conform to our human expectations. The poor in spirit, not the rich, inherit the kingdom of heaven. We must lose our life for the Lord's sake in order to gain it eternally. And as the Apostle Paul expresses our present theme, "Whenever I am weak, then I am strong" (2 Cor 12:10).

Paul's point is that when we are weak in our own human strength, Christ is able to fill us with His supernatural strength. He can then use us in extraordinary ways. That's precisely why Paul could even boast of his weaknesses, and St. Faustina could tell Jesus, "I want to worship You with my very weakness" (*Diary*, 782).

STRENGTH *and* WEAKNESS

55. Not on Your Own Strength

On its own strength, the soul will not go far; it will exert itself greatly and will do nothing for the glory of God; it will err continually, because our mind is darkened and does not know how to discern its own affairs.

— Diary, 377

I do not understand my own actions. For I do not do what I want, but I do the very thing I hate. ... Wretched man that I am! Who will rescue me from this body of death? Thanks be to God through Jesus Christ our Lord!

— Romans 7:15, 24-25

56. 'I Can Do All Things'

A soul cannot do much of itself, but with God it can do all things. ... When I see that the burden is beyond my strength, I do not consider or analyze it or probe into it, but I run like a child to the Heart of Jesus and say only one word to Him: "You can do all things." And then I keep silent, because I know that Jesus Himself will intervene in the matter, and as for me, instead of tormenting myself, I use that time to love Him.

— Diary, 138, 1033

"For God all things are possible." ... I can do all things through him who strengthens me.

— Mark 10:27; Philippians 4:13

57. The Cause of Lapses

When one day I resolved to practice a certain virtue, I lapsed into the vice opposed to that virtue ten times more frequently than on other days. In the evening, I was reflecting on why, today, I had lapsed so extraordinarily, and I heard the words: **You were counting too much on yourself and too little on Me.** And I understood the cause of my lapses.

— *Diary*, 1087

For not by their own sword did they win the land, nor did their own arm give them victory; but your right hand, and your arm, and the light of your countenance, for you delighted in them.

— Psalm 44:3

58. Worship with Weakness

I am very weak today. I cannot even make my meditation in the chapel, but must lie down. O my Jesus, I love You, and I want to worship You with my very weakness, submitting myself entirely to Your holy will.

— *Diary*, 782

I will boast all the more gladly of my weaknesses, so that the power of Christ may dwell in me. Therefore I am content with weaknesses, insults, hardships, persecutions, and calamities for the sake of Christ; for whenever I am weak, then I am strong.

— 2 Corinthians 12:9-10

59. 'Name of Jesus'

The Name of Jesus. Oh, how great is Your Name, O Lord! It is the strength of my soul. When my strength fails, and darkness invades my soul, Your Name is the sun whose rays give light and also warmth, and under their influence the soul becomes more beautiful and radiant, taking its splendor from Your Name. When I hear the sweetest Name of Jesus, my heartbeat grows stronger.

— Diary, 862

At the name of Jesus every knee should bend, in heaven and on earth and under the earth, and every tongue should confess that Jesus Christ is Lord, to the glory of God the Father.

— Philippians 2:10-11

60. 'Speaking the Truth'

O my Jesus, You know that I have gotten myself into a lot of trouble for speaking out the truth. O truth, so often oppressed, you nearly always wear a crown of thorns! O Eternal Truth, support me that I may have the courage to speak the truth even if it would come about that I would pay for it with my life. O Jesus, how hard it is to believe in this, when one sees one thing taught and something else lived.

— Diary, 1482

Speaking the truth in love, we must grow up in every way into him who is the head, into Christ. … So then, putting away falsehood, let all of us speak the truth to our neighbors, for we are members of one another.

— Ephesians 4:15, 25

My Reflections
on the Theme

My Reflections
on the Theme

The PASSION *of* CHRIST

Journey with Jesus to Calvary. Read the Gospel accounts alongside St. Faustina's Diary entries, which tell the remarkable story of how the Lord granted her a small share in His Passion. She writes of the profound impact these mystical experiences had on her soul, "In the course of this suffering, my love grew immeasurably. ... The world still has no idea of all that Jesus suffered" (*Diary*, 1054). In fact, St. Faustina came to abhor "even the smallest sin," knowing how much it had cost Jesus during His Passion (*Diary*, 1016).

As you reflect on the Passion, consider your own sins. Make a firm resolution to detest and avoid them out of love for the Lord.

The PASSION of CHRIST

61. The Agony

I entered into the sufferings which Jesus underwent in the Garden of Olives. ... The Lord pressed me to His Heart and said, **I shall give you a small portion of My Passion.** ... When Jesus was taking leave of me, such great pain filled my soul that it is impossible to express it. ... Every beat of Jesus' Heart was reflected in my heart and pierced my soul. ... In the course of this suffering, my love grew immeasurably. ... Together with Him, I underwent, in a special way, all the various tortures. The world still has no idea of all that Jesus suffered. I accompanied Him to the Garden of Gethsemane. ... I came to know all the omnipotence of His love and of His mercy toward souls.

— Diary, 646, 1053-1054

Then Jesus came with them to a place called Gethsemane. ... He took along Peter and the two sons of Zebedee, and began to feel sorrow and distress. Then he said to them, "My soul is sorrowful even to death." ... He was in such agony and he prayed so fervently that his sweat became like drops of blood falling on the ground.

— Matthew 26:36-38 (NAB); Luke 22:44 (NAB)

62. 'The Scourging'

I saw the Lord Jesus tied to a pillar, stripped of His clothes, and the scourging began immediately. ... I saw how the Lord Jesus suffered as He was being scourged. Oh, such an inconceivable agony! ... His blood flowed to the ground, and in some places His flesh started to fall off. I saw a few bare bones on His back. The meek Jesus moaned softly and sighed. ... My heart almost stopped at the sight of these tortures. The Lord said to me, **I suffer even greater pain than that which you see.** And Jesus gave me to know for what sins He subjected himself to the scourging: these are sins of impurity. Oh, how dreadful was Jesus' moral suffering during the scourging!

— Diary, 445, 188

Then Pilate took Jesus and had him scourged. ... But he was pierced for our sins, crushed for our iniquity. He bore the punishment that makes us whole, by his wounds we were healed.

— John 19:1 (NAB); Isaiah 53:5 (NAB)

63. The Crowning

After the scourging, the torturers took the Lord and stripped Him of His own garment, which had already adhered to the wounds; as they took it off, His wounds reopened; then they threw a dirty and tattered scarlet cloak over the fresh wounds of the Lord. … Then they wove a crown of thorns, which they put on His sacred head. They put a reed in His hand and made fun of Him, bowing to Him as to a king. Some spat in His face, while others took the reed and struck Him on the head with it. Others caused him pain by slapping Him; still others covered His face and struck Him with their fists. Jesus bore all this with meekness. Who can comprehend Him — comprehend His suffering?

— Diary, 408

The soldiers wove a crown of thorns and put it on his head, and they dressed him in a purple robe. They kept coming up to him, saying, "Hail, King of the Jews!" and striking him on the face. Pilate went out again and said to them, "Look, I am bringing him out to you to let you know that I find no case against him." … When the chief priests and the police saw him, they shouted, "Crucify him! Crucify him!"

— John 19:2-4, 6

64. Carrying the Cross

I saw a multitude of souls crucified like Him. Then I saw a second multitude of souls, and a third. The second multitude were not nailed to [their] crosses, but were holding them firmly in their hands. The third were neither nailed to [their] crosses nor holding them firmly in their hands, but were dragging [their] crosses behind them and were discontent. Jesus then said to me, **Do you see these souls? Those who are like Me in the pain and contempt they suffer will be like Me also in glory. And those who resemble Me less in pain and contempt will also bear less resemblance to Me in glory.**

— Diary, 446

"I am the way, and the truth, and the life." … "Whoever wishes to come after me must deny himself, take up his cross, and follow me. For whoever wishes to save his life will lose it, but whoever loses his life for my sake will find it."

— John 14:6; Matthew 16:24-25 (NAB)

65. The Crucifixion

I saw the Lord Jesus nailed upon the cross amidst great torments.
A soft moan issued from His Heart. After some time, He said, **I
thirst. I thirst for the salvation of souls. Help Me, My
daughter, to save souls. Join your sufferings to My Passion
and offer them to the heavenly Father for sinners.** ... I then
felt in my soul the desire to save souls and to empty myself for the
sake of poor sinners. I offered myself, together with the dying
Jesus, to the Eternal Father, for the salvation of the whole world.

— *Diary*, 1032, 648

After this, aware that everything was now finished, in order that
the scripture might be fulfilled, Jesus said, "I thirst." There was
a vessel filled with common wine. So they put a sponge soaked
in wine on a sprig of hyssop and put it up to his mouth. When
Jesus had taken the wine, he said, "It is finished." And bowing
his head, he handed over the spirit.

— John 19:28-30 (NAB)

66. Not Even the Least Sin

Today, I entered into the bitterness of the Passion of the Lord
Jesus. ... I learned in the depths of my soul how horrible sin was,
even the smallest sin, and how much it tormented the soul of Jesus.
... O my Jesus, I would rather be in agony until the end of the
world, amidst the greatest sufferings, than offend You by the least
sin. ... I fear only one thing, and that is to offend You. My Jesus,
I would rather not exist than make You sad.

— *Diary*, 1016, 741, 571

The death he died, he died to sin, once for all; but the life he
lives, he lives to God. So you also must consider yourselves dead
to sin and alive to God in Christ Jesus.

— Romans 6:10-11

My Reflections
on the Theme

My Reflections
on the Theme

The CALL to SINNERS

We should be quick every day to confess our sins. After all, even "the just man falls seven times and rises again [every day]" (Prov 24:16). The important thing is that we turn back to the Lord. In fact, Jesus is so merciful that He told St. Faustina, **"I cannot punish even the greatest sinner if he makes an appeal to My compassion"** (*Diary*, 1146).

Yet the Day of Justice is also approaching, which is why the message of Divine Mercy is so urgent. As Jesus told St. Faustina, **"Speak to the world about My mercy ... . While there is still time, let them have recourse to the fount of My mercy"** (*Diary*, 848). Are we listening?

The CALL to SINNERS

67. Appeal to His Mercy

[Let] the greatest sinners place their trust in My mercy. They have the right before others to trust in the abyss of My mercy. My daughter, write about My mercy towards tormented souls. Souls that make an appeal to My mercy delight Me. To such souls I grant even more graces than they ask. I cannot punish even the greatest sinner if he makes an appeal to My compassion.

— Diary, 1146

"Those who are well have no need of a physician, but those who are sick. Go and learn what this means, 'I desire mercy, not sacrifice.' For I have come to call not the righteous but sinners."

— Matthew 9:12-13

68. No Sin Too Great

Let no soul fear to draw near to Me, even though its sins be as scarlet. ... The greatest sinners would achieve great sanctity, if only they would trust in My mercy. The very inner depths of My being are filled to overflowing with mercy, and it is being poured out upon all I have created.

— Diary, 699, 1784

Though your sins be like scarlet, they may become white as snow; though they be crimson red, they may become white as wool.

— Isaiah 1:18 (NAB)

69. No One Excluded

Today the Lord said to me, ... **The greater the misery of a soul, the greater its right to My mercy; [urge] all souls to trust in the unfathomable abyss of My mercy, because I want to save them all. On the cross, the fountain of My mercy was opened wide by the lance for all souls — no one have I excluded!**

— Diary, 1182

"And when I am lifted up from the earth, I will draw everyone to myself."

— John 12:32 (NAB)

70. Even in Punishment

O my God, even in the punishments You send down upon the earth I see the abyss of Your mercy, for by punishing us here on earth You free us from eternal punishment. Rejoice, all you creatures, for you are closer to God in His infinite mercy than a baby to its mother's heart.

— Diary, 423

My child, do not despise the Lord's discipline or be weary of his reproof, for the Lord reproves the one he loves, as a father the son in whom he delights. ... Therefore do not despise the discipline of the Almighty. For he wounds, but he binds up; he strikes, but his hands heal.

— Proverbs 3:11-12; Job 5:17-18

71. 'Day of Justice'

I heard a voice which said, ... **Speak to the world about My mercy ... . It is a sign for the end times. ... While there is still time, let them have recourse to the fount of My mercy. ... Before the day of justice arrives, there will be given to people a sign in the heavens ... All light in the heavens will be extinguished, and there will be great darkness over the whole earth. Then the sign of the cross will be seen in the sky, and from the openings where the hands and the feet of the Savior were nailed will come forth great lights which will light up the earth.**

— Diary, 848, 83

"The sun will be darkened, and the moon will not give its light; the stars will fall from heaven, and the powers of heaven will be shaken." ... "They will see the Son of Man coming on the clouds of heaven with power and great glory. And he will send out his angels with a loud trumpet call, and they will gather his elect from the four winds, from one end of heaven to the other."

— Matthew 24:29-31

72. Hide in His Mercy

I saw the Mother of God, who said to me, ... *I gave the Savior to the world; as for you, you have to speak to the world about His great mercy and prepare the world for the Second Coming of Him who will come, not as a merciful Savior, but as a just Judge. Oh, how terrible is that day! Determined is the day of justice, the day of divine wrath. ... Speak to souls about this great mercy while it is still the time for [granting] mercy. ...* O human souls, where are you going to hide on the day of God's anger? Take refuge now in the fount of God's mercy.

— Diary, 635, 848

I looked, and there came a great earthquake; the sun became black as sackcloth, the full moon became like blood, and the stars of the sky fell to the earth. ... Then the kings of the earth and the magnates and the generals and the rich and the powerful, and everyone, slave and free, hid in the caves and among the rocks of the mountains, calling to the mountains and rocks, "Fall on us and hide us from the face of the one seated on the throne and from the wrath of the Lamb; for the great day of their wrath has come, and who is able to stand?"

— Revelation 6:12-13, 15-17

My Reflections
on the Theme

My Reflections
on the Theme

GRACE

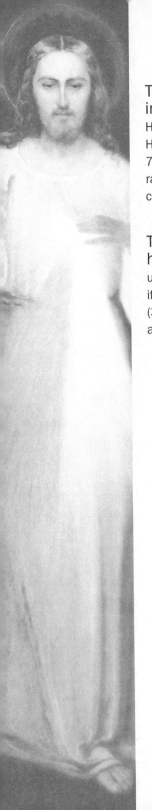

The Merciful Savior cannot be outdone in generosity. When we place our trust in Him, He literally showers us with graces from the fount of His mercy (among many *Diary* passages, see 699, 793, and 848). Jesus also uses the image of us radiating these graces out to others, since we cannot contain them in ourselves (see *Diary*, 1074).

The problem comes when we harden our hearts, because the Lord will not force His graces upon us. As the writer to the Hebrews tells us, "Today, if you hear his voice, do not harden your hearts" (3:15). So make a habit of turning to the Lord with trust and asking Him to soften your heart.

GRACE

73. Radiating Grace

When I went for adoration, I heard these words: ...Tell aching **mankind to snuggle close to My merciful Heart, and I will fill it with peace. ... I am Love and Mercy itself. When a soul approaches Me with trust, I fill it with such an abundance of graces that it cannot contain them within itself, but radiates them to other souls.**

— Diary, 1074

From his fullness we have all received, grace upon grace. ... Look to God that you may be radiant with joy. ... May the Lord make you increase and abound in love for one another and for all, just as we abound in love for you.

— John 1:16; Psalm 34:5 (NAB); 1 Thessalonians 3:12

74. 'Set Ajar the Door'

The last hour abounds with mercy for us. Let no one doubt concerning the goodness of God; even if a person's sins were as dark as night, God's mercy is stronger than our misery. One thing alone is necessary: that the sinner set ajar the door of his heart, be it ever so little, to let in a ray of God's merciful grace. ... Then the mercy of God begins to exert itself, and, without any co-operation from the soul, God grants it final grace. If this too is spurned, God will leave the soul in this self-chosen disposition for eternity. ... The soul knows that this, for her, is final grace and, should it show even a flicker of good will, the mercy of God will accomplish the rest.

— Diary, 1507, 1486

"Be earnest, therefore, and repent. Listen! I am standing at the door, knocking; if you hear my voice and open the door, I will come in to you and eat with you, and you with me."

— Revelation 3:19-20

75. 'Final Grace'

God's mercy sometimes touches the sinner at the last moment in a wondrous and mysterious way. Outwardly, it seems as if everything were lost, but it is not so. The soul, illumined by a ray of God's powerful final grace, turns to God in the last moment with such a power of love that, in an instant, it receives from God forgiveness of sin and punishment, while outwardly it shows no sign either of repentance or of contrition. ... Although a person is at the point of death, the merciful God gives the soul that interior vivid moment, so that if the soul is willing, it has the possibility of returning to God. But sometimes, the obduracy in souls is so great that consciously they choose hell; they [thus] make useless all the prayers that other souls offer to God for them and even the efforts of God Himself.

— Diary, 1698

Take care, brothers and sisters, that none of you may have an evil, unbelieving heart that turns away from the living God ... that none of you may be hardened by the deceitfulness of sin. ... Today, if you hear his voice, do not harden your hearts.

— Hebrews 3:12-13, 15

My Reflections
on the Theme

HOLINESS

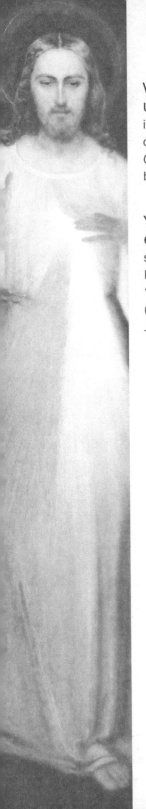

Vatican II clearly teaches that there is a universal call to holiness: "... all Christians in any state or walk of life are called to the fullness of Christian life and to the perfection of love" (*Lumen Gentium*, 40). As the Lord Himself tells us, "You shall be holy, for I am holy" (1 Pet 1:16).

Yet we can become discouraged about ever achieving holiness as we struggle with our sins. Saint Faustina assures us that all we need is "a bit of good will," and then Jesus will hurry to help us. "Indeed, He gives us more than what we ask of Him" (*Diary*, 291). So let's start with our good will and trust Jesus to do the rest.

HOLINESS

76. Called to Sanctity

Let no soul, even the most miserable, fall prey to doubt; for, as long as one is alive, each one can become a great saint, so great is the power of God's grace. It remains only for us not to oppose God's action. ... The holiness of God is poured out upon the Church of God and upon every living soul in it, but not in the same degree. There are souls who are completely penetrated by God, and there are those who are barely alive.

— Diary, 283, 180

Like obedient children, do not be conformed to the desires that you formerly had in ignorance. Instead, as he who called you is holy, be holy yourselves in all your conduct; for it is written, "You shall be holy, for I am holy."

— 1 Peter 1:14-16

77. Faithful to Grace

How very easy it is to become holy; all that is needed is a bit of good will. If Jesus sees this little bit of good will in the soul, He hurries to give Himself to the soul, and nothing can stop Him, neither shortcomings nor falls — absolutely nothing. Jesus is anxious to help that soul, and if it is faithful to this grace from God, it can very soon attain the highest holiness possible for a creature here on earth. God is very generous and does not deny His grace to anyone. Indeed, He gives more than what we ask of Him. Faithfulness to the inspirations of the Holy Spirit — that is the shortest route.

— Diary, 291

Blessed be the God and Father of our Lord Jesus Christ, who has blessed us in Christ with every spiritual blessing in the heavenly places, just as he chose us in Christ before the foundation of the world to be holy and blameless before him in love.

— Ephesians 1:3-4

78. 'Strive for Perfection'

I heard a voice in my soul: … **If you strive for perfection you will sanctify many souls; and if you do not strive for sanctity, by the same token, many souls will remain imperfect. Know that their perfection will depend on your perfection, and the greater part of the responsibility for these souls will fall on you.**

— *Diary*, 1163, 1165

"Be perfect, just as your heavenly Father is perfect." … Strive for peace with everyone, and for that holiness without which no one will see the Lord.

— Matthew 5:48 (NAB); Hebrews 12:14 (NAB)

79. Transformation

I want to be completely transformed into Your mercy and to be Your living reflection, O Lord. May the greatest of all divine attributes, that of Your unfathomable mercy, pass through my heart and soul to my neighbor.

— *Diary*, 163

Do not be conformed to this world, but be transformed by the renewing of your minds. … Put away your former way of life, your old self, corrupt and deluded by its lusts, and … clothe yourselves with the new self, created according to the likeness of God in true righteousness and holiness.

— Romans 12:2; Ephesians 4:22, 24

80. 'Do Not Judge'

Today, I was talking with the Lord, and He said to me, **There are souls with whom I can do nothing. They are souls that are continuously observing others, but know nothing of what is going on within their own selves. They talk about others continually. ... Poor souls, they do not hear My words; their interior remains empty. They do not look for Me within their own hearts, but in idle talk, where I am never to be found. They sense their emptiness, but they do not recognize their own guilt.**

— Diary, 1717

"Do not judge, so that you may not be judged. For with the judgment you make you will be judged, and the measure you give will be the measure you get. Why do you see the speck in your neighbor's eye, but do not notice the log in your own eye? Or how can you say to your neighbor, 'Let me take the speck out of your eye,' while the log is in your own eye? You hypocrite, first take the log out of your own eye, and then you will see clearly to take the speck out of your neighbor's eye."

— Matthew 7:1-5

81. 'The Present Moment'

I waste no time in dreaming. I take every moment singly as it comes, for this is within my power. The past does not belong to me; the future is not mine; with all my soul I try to make use of the present moment. ... O Jesus, I want to live in the present moment, to live as if this were the last day of my life. I want to use every moment scrupulously for the greater glory of God, to use every circumstance for the benefit of my soul. I want to look upon everything, from the point of view that nothing happens without the will of God.

— Diary, 351, 1183

"Do not worry about tomorrow, for tomorrow will bring worries of its own. Today's trouble is enough for today."

— Matthew 6:34

82. Violet in the Grass

I will hide from people's eyes whatever good I am able to do so that God Himself may be my reward. I will be like a tiny violet hidden in the grass, which does not hurt the foot that treads on it, but diffuses its fragrance and, forgetting itself completely, tries to please the person who has crushed it underfoot. This is very difficult for human nature, but God's grace comes to one's aid.

— Diary, 255

"Beware of practicing your piety before others in order to be seen by them; for then you have no reward from your Father in heaven. So whenever you give alms, do not sound a trumpet before you, as the hypocrites do in the synagogues and in the streets, so that they may be praised by others. Truly I tell you, they have received their reward. But when you give alms, do not let your left hand know what your right hand is doing, so that your alms may be done in secret; and your Father who sees in secret will reward you."

— Matthew 6:1-4

83. 'Purity'

Jesus appeared suddenly at my side clad in a white garment with a golden girdle around His waist, and He said to me, **I give you eternal love that your purity may be untarnished and as a sign that you will never be subject to temptations against purity.** Jesus took off His golden cincture and tied it around my waist. Since then I have never experienced any attacks against this virtue, either in my heart or in my mind. I later understood that this was one of the greatest graces which the Most Holy Virgin Mary had obtained for me, as for many years I had been asking this grace of her.

— Diary, 40

This is the will of God, your holiness: that you refrain from immorality. ... For God did not call us to impurity but to holiness. ... Create in me a clean heart, O God, and put a new and right spirit within me.

— 1 Thessalonians 4:3,7 (NAB); Psalm 51:10

My Reflections
on the Theme

LOVED *in the* WOMB *and* MARY

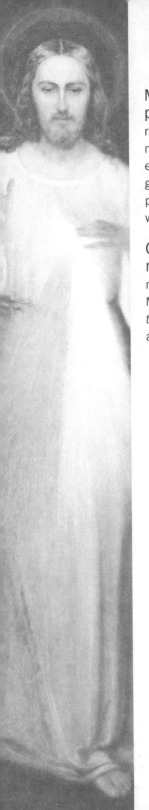

Many of us carry deep wounds from a painful upbringing. Healing can begin when we realize that God knew us before He formed us in our mother's womb. He has loved each of us "with an everlasting love" (Is 54:10). As we ponder God's great love in creating us, we can exclaim like the psalmist, "I praise you, so wonderfully you made me; wonderful are your works!" (Ps 139:14).

God also knew we needed a spiritual mother, so Jesus from the Cross gave us His own mother (see Jn 19:26-27). Indeed, the Blessed Virgin Mary told St. Faustina, "*I am a Mother to you all, thanks to the unfathomable mercy of God*" (*Diary*, 449). What a precious gift!

LOVED *in the* WOMB

84. 'I Thought of You'

When I received Holy Communion, I said to Him, "Jesus, I thought about You so many times last night," and Jesus answered me, **And I thought of you before I called you into being. … Before I made the world, I loved you with the love your heart is experiencing today and, throughout the centuries, My love will never change.**

— Diary, 1292, 1754

Before I formed you in the womb I knew you. … I have loved you with an everlasting love. … The mountains may depart and the hills be removed, but my steadfast love shall not depart from you … Thus says the Lord who made you, who formed you in the womb.

— Jeremiah 1:5; 31:3; Isaiah 54:10; 44:2

85. Reparation for Abortion

At eight o'clock I was seized with such violent pains that I had to go to bed at once. I was convulsed with pain for three hours; … At times, the pains caused me to lose consciousness. Jesus had me realize that in this way I took part in His Agony in the Garden, and that He Himself allowed these sufferings in order to offer reparation to God for the souls murdered in the wombs …. I have gone through these sufferings three times now. They always start at eight o'clock in the evening and last until eleven. No medicine can lessen these sufferings. … I don't know whether I'll ever again suffer in this way; I leave that to God. What it pleases God to send, I will accept with submission and love. If only I could save even one soul from murder by means of these sufferings!

— Diary, 1276

I call heaven and earth to witness against you today that I have set before you life and death, blessings and curses. Choose life, so that you and your descendants may live.

— Deuteronomy 30:19

MARY

86. Mother to All

I saw the Blessed Virgin, unspeakably beautiful. She came down from the altar to my kneeler, held me close to herself and said to me, *I am Mother to you all, thanks to the unfathomable mercy of God.* … Smiling at me she said to me, *My daughter, at God's command I am to be, in a special and exclusive way your Mother; but I desire that you, too, in a special way, be my child.*

— *Diary*, 449, 1414

When Jesus saw his mother and the disciple whom he loved standing beside her, he said to his mother, "Woman, here is your son." Then he said to the disciple, "Here is your mother." And from that hour the disciple took her into his own home.

— John 19:26-27

87. Mary Taught Me

I have experienced an increasing devotion to the Mother of God. She has taught me how to love God interiorly and also how to carry out His holy will in all things.

— *Diary*, 40

His mother said to the servants, "Do whatever he tells you."

— John 2:5

My Reflections
on the Theme

PRAYER

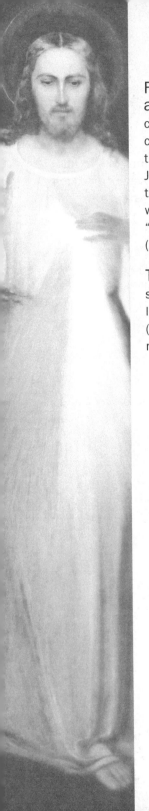

For Christians, prayer should be the very air we breathe. Jesus points the way through His constant communion of prayer with the Father. This constant prayer with the Father is implied throughout the Gospel of John. For instance, Jesus tells the Jews, "I do nothing on my own, but I say only what the Father has taught me. The one who sent me is with me" (Jn 8:28-29). So, too, St. Faustina advises, "In whatever state a soul may be, it ought to pray" (*Diary*, 146).

To help you breathe spiritually, here are some key lessons on prayer. Note especially the final lesson on taking a break from "the whirl of work" (*Diary*, 226). It's a lesson the Marthas among us need to take to heart (see LK 10:38-42).

PRAYER

88. Conversion Prayer

The Lord said to me, **The loss of each soul plunges Me into mortal sadness. You always console Me when you pray for sinners. The prayer most pleasing to Me is prayer for the conversion of sinners. ... This prayer is always heard and answered. ... When you say this prayer, with a contrite heart and with faith on behalf of some sinner, I will give him the grace of conversion. This is the prayer: "O Blood and Water, which gushed forth from the Heart of Jesus as a fount of Mercy for us, I trust in You."**

— *Diary*, 1397, 186-187

"I will do whatever you ask in my name, so that the Father may be glorified in the Son. If in my name you ask me for anything, I will do it". ... "It is not the will of your Father in heaven that one of these little ones should be lost."

— John 14:13-14; Matthew 18:14

89. 'Pray in the Spirit'

I saw the Mother of God, unspeakably beautiful. She said to me, *My daughter, what I demand from you is prayer, prayer, and once again prayer, for the world and especially for your country. ... At all times and places, day or night, whenever you wake up, pray in the spirit. In spirit, one can always remain in prayer.*

— *Diary*, 325

Pray in the Spirit at all times in every prayer and supplication.

— Ephesians 6:18

90. 'Bound to Pray'

In whatever state the soul may be, it ought to pray. A soul which is pure and beautiful must pray, or else it will lose its beauty; a soul which is striving after this purity must pray, or else it will never attain it; a soul which is newly converted must pray, or else it will fall again; a sinful soul, plunged in sins, must pray so that it might rise again. There is no soul which is not bound to pray, for every single grace comes to the soul through prayer.

— *Diary*, 146

Do not worry about anything, but in everything by prayer and supplication with thanksgiving let your requests be made known to God.

— Philippians 4:6

91. Saving Others

We do not know the number of souls that is ours to save through our prayers and sacrifices; therefore, let us always pray for sinners.

— *Diary*, 1783

The prayer of the righteous is powerful and effective. ... My brothers and sisters, if anyone among you wanders from the truth and is brought back by another, you should know that whoever brings back a sinner from wandering will save the sinner's soul from death and will cover a multitude of sins.

— James 5:16, 19-20

92. Perseverance in Prayer

Jesus gave me to understand how a soul should be faithful to prayer despite torments, dryness and temptations; because oftentimes the realization of God's great plans depends mainly on such prayer. If we do not persevere in such prayer, we frustrate what the Lord wanted to do through us or within us.

— Diary, 872

Then Jesus told them a parable about their need to pray always. … He said, "In a certain city there was a judge who neither feared God nor had respect for people. … There was a widow who kept coming to him and saying, 'Grant me justice against my opponent.' … He said to himself, 'Though I have no fear of God and no respect for anyone, yet because this widow keeps bothering me, I will grant her justice, so that she may not wear me out by continually coming.'" And the Lord said, "Listen to what the unjust judge says. And will not God grant justice to his chosen ones who cry to him day and night? Will he delay long in helping them? I tell you, he will quickly grant justice to them."

— Luke 18:1-8

93. 'Take a Break'

I must not let myself become absorbed in the whirl of work, [but] take a break to look up to heaven. … I will not allow myself to be so absorbed in the whirlwind of work as to forget about God. I will spend all my free moments at the feet of the Master hidden in the Blessed Sacrament. He has been tutoring me from my most tender years.

— Diary, 226, 82

Now as they went on their way, he entered a certain village, where a woman named Martha welcomed him into her home. She had a sister named Mary, who sat at the Lord's feet and listened to what he was saying. But Martha was distracted by her many tasks; so she came to him and asked, "Lord, do you not care that my sister has left me to do all the work by myself? Tell her then to help me." But the Lord answered her, "Martha, Martha, you are worried and distracted by many things; there is need of only one thing. Mary has chosen the better part, which will not be taken away from her."

— Luke 10:38-42

My Reflections
on the Theme

My Reflections
on the Theme

HEAVEN, HELL, *and* SPIRITUAL WARFARE

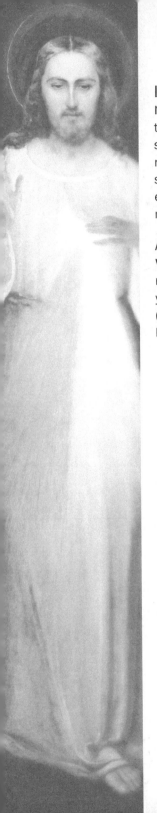

If possible, take more time to ponder the meaning of these more serious passages. With the passages on heaven, be encouraged. Let your spirit soar with praises to God's throne, accompanied by the angels and saints. With the ones on hell, soberly consider its existence for those who reject God, especially given St. Faustina's chilling observation that most of the souls in hell didn't believe it existed.

As you turn to the passages on spiritual warfare, consciously don the armor that St. Paul mentions in Ephesians 6 and ask our Lord to help you fight "like a knight" for souls, as St. Faustina did (*Diary*, 1760). In the heat of battle, know that you have the victory in Jesus' name!

HEAVEN

94. 'Eye Has Not Seen'

November 27, [1936]. Today I was in heaven, in spirit, and I saw its inconceivable beauties and the happiness that awaits us after death. I saw how all creatures give ceaseless praise and glory to God. I saw how great is happiness in God, which spreads to all creatures, making them happy; and then all the glory and praise which springs from this happiness returns to its source; and they enter into the depths of God, contemplating the inner life of God, the Father, the Son, and the Holy Spirit, whom they will never comprehend or fathom.

— Diary, 777

What eye has not seen, and ear has not heard, and what has not entered the human heart, what God has prepared for those who love him, this God has revealed to us through the Spirit. ... At present we see indistinctly, as in a mirror, but then face to face.

— 1 Corinthians 2:9-10; 13:12 (NAB)

HELL

95. Faustina's Visit

Today, I was led by an Angel to the chasms of hell. ... Each soul undergoes terrible and indescribable sufferings, related to the manner in which it has sinned. There are caverns and pits of torture where one form of agony differs from another. ... Let the sinner know that he will be tortured throughout all eternity, in those senses which he made use of to sin. I am writing this at the command of God, so that no soul may find an excuse by saying there is no hell. ... I, Sister Faustina, by the order of God, have visited the abysses of hell so that I might tell souls about it and testify to its existence. ... Most of the souls there are those who disbelieved that there is a hell.

— Diary, 741

The devil who had deceived them was thrown into the lake of fire and sulfur, where the beast and the false prophet were, and they will be tormented day and night for ever and ever. ... The dead were judged according to their works. ... All were judged according to what they had done. ... Anyone whose name was not found written in the book of life was thrown into the lake of fire. ... As for the cowardly, the faithless, the polluted, the murderers, the fornicators, the sorcerers, the idolaters, and all liars, their place will be in the lake that burns with fire and sulfur, which is the second death.

— Revelation 20:10, 12-15; 21:8

SPIRITUAL WARFARE

96. Glory to God Alone

During the night, a soul I had already seen before visited me. However, it did not ask for prayer, but reproached me, saying that I used to be very haughty and vain ... "and now you are interceding for others while you yourself still have certain vices." ... The soul continued to reproach me, saying, "Why are you unwilling to recognize my greatness? Why do you alone not glorify me for my great deeds as all others do?" Then I saw that this was Satan under the assumed appearance of this soul and I said, "Glory is due to God alone; be gone, Satan!" And in an instant this soul fell into an abyss, horrible beyond all description.

— Diary, 520

Then the devil led him up and showed him in an instant all the kingdoms of the world. And the devil said to him, "To you I will give their glory and all this authority; for it has been given over to me, and I give it to anyone I please. If you, then, will worship me, it will all be yours." Jesus answered him, "It is written, 'Worship the Lord your God, and serve only him.'"

— Luke 4:5-8

97. 'Fight like a Knight'

My daughter, I want to teach you about spiritual warfare. Never trust in yourself, but abandon yourself totally to My will. In desolation, darkness and various doubts, have recourse to Me and to your spiritual director. ... Do not bargain with any temptation; lock yourself immediately in My Heart and, at the first opportunity, reveal the temptation to the confessor. ... Do not fear struggle; courage itself often intimidates temptations, and they dare not attack us. Always fight with the deep conviction that I am with you. ... Prepare for great battles. Know that you are now on a great stage where all heaven and earth are watching you. Fight like a knight, so that I can reward you. Do not be unduly fearful, because you are not alone.

— Diary, 1760

Put on the whole armor of God, so that you may be able to stand against the wiles of the devil. For our struggle is not against enemies of blood and flesh, but against the rulers, against the authorities, against the cosmic powers of this present darkness, against the spiritual forces of evil in the heavenly places. Therefore take up the whole armor of God. ...Fasten the belt of truth around your waist, and put on the breastplate of righteousness. ... Take the shield of faith, with which you will be able to quench all the flaming arrows of the evil one. Take the helmet of salvation, and the sword of the Spirit, which is the word of God.

— Ephesians 6:11-14, 16-17

My Reflections
on the Theme

MERCY, MY HOPE

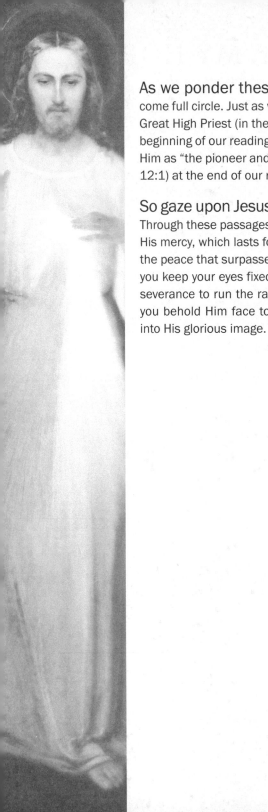

As we ponder these last passages, we've come full circle. Just as we gazed upon Jesus as the Great High Priest (in the Divine Mercy Image) at the beginning of our readings, so now we fix our eyes on Him as "the pioneer and perfecter of our faith" (Heb 12:1) at the end of our readings.

So gaze upon Jesus and receive His gaze. Through these passages, know that you can hope in His mercy, which lasts forever. Only He can give you the peace that surpasses all understanding. And as you keep your eyes fixed on Him, He'll give you perseverance to run the race. Don't stop running until you behold Him face to face and are transformed into His glorious image.

MERCY, MY HOPE

98. Mercy Is Forever

Let every soul trust in the Passion of the Lord, and place its hope in His mercy. God will not deny His mercy to anyone. Heaven and earth may change, but God's mercy will never be exhausted.

— *Diary*, 72

For the Lord is good; his steadfast love endures forever, and his faithfulness to all generations.

— Psalm 100:5

99. Trust in Mercy Gives Us Peace

Mankind will not have peace until it turns with trust to My mercy. ... Tell aching mankind to snuggle close to My merciful Heart, and I will fill it with peace.

— *Diary*, 300, 1074

Jesus came and stood among them and said, "Peace be with you." ... "Peace I leave with you; my peace I give to you. I do not give to you as the world gives. Do not let your hearts be troubled, and do not let them be afraid." ... The peace of God, which surpasses all understanding, will guard your hearts and your minds in Christ Jesus.

— John 20:19; 14:27; Philippians 4:7

100. Eyes Fixed on Christ

Amid the greatest torments, I fix the gaze of my soul upon Jesus Crucified; I do not expect help from people, but place my trust in God. In His unfathomable mercy lies all my hope.

— Diary, 681

Let us run with perseverance the race that is set before us, looking to Jesus the pioneer and perfecter of our faith, who for the sake of the joy that was set before him endured the cross, disregarding its shame, and has taken his seat at the right hand of the throne of God.

— Hebrews 12:1-2

My Reflections
on the Theme

APPENDIX:

MERCY PRAYERS *from*
SCRIPTURE *and the*
DIARY OF ST. FAUSTINA

PRAYERS *from* SCRIPTURE

Jacob's Prayer, Genesis 32:9-12

"O God of my father Abraham and God of my father Isaac, O Lord who didst say to me, 'Return to your country and to your kindred, and I will do you good,' I am not worthy of the least of all the steadfast love and all the faithfulness which thou hast shown to thy servant, for with only my staff I crossed this Jordan; and now I have become two companies. Deliver me, I pray thee, from the hand of my brother, from the hand of Esau, for I fear him, lest he come and slay us all, the mothers with the children. But thou didst say, 'I will do you good, and make your descendants as the sand of the sea, which cannot be numbered for multitude.'"

Hannah's Prayer, 1 Samuel 2:1-10
Hannah's Prayer is considered a prototype of Mary's Magnificat.

My heart exults in the Lord;
  my strength is exalted in the Lord.
My mouth derides my enemies,
  because I rejoice in thy salvation.
"There is none holy like the Lord,
  there is none besides thee;
  there is no rock like our God.
Talk no more so very proudly,
  let not arrogance come from your mouth;
for the Lord is a God of knowledge,
  and by him actions are weighed.
The bows of the mighty are broken,
  but the feeble gird on strength.
Those who were full have hired themselves out for bread,
  but those who were hungry have ceased to hunger.
The barren has borne seven,
  but she who has many children is forlorn.
The Lord kills and brings to life;
  he brings down to Sheol and raises up.
The Lord makes poor and makes rich;

he brings low, he also exalts.
He raises up the poor from the dust;
 he lifts the needy from the ash heap,
to make them sit with princes
 and inherit a seat of honor.
For the pillars of the earth are the Lord's,
 and on them he has set the world.
"He will guard the feet of his faithful ones;
 but the wicked shall be cut off in darkness;
 for not by might shall a man prevail.
The adversaries of the Lord shall be broken to pieces;
 against them he will thunder in heaven.
The Lord will judge the ends of the earth;
 he will give strength to his king,
 and exalt the power of his anointed."

Nehemiah's Prayer, Nehemiah 1:5-11

"O Lord God of heaven, the great and terrible God who keeps covenant and steadfast love with those who love him and keep his commandments; let thy ear be attentive, and thy eyes open, to hear the prayer of thy servant which I now pray before thee day and night for the people of Israel thy servants, confessing the sins of the people of Israel, which we have sinned against thee. Yea, I and my father's house have sinned. We have acted very corruptly against thee, and have not kept the commandments, the statutes, and the ordinances which thou didst command thy servant Moses. Remember the word which thou didst command thy servant Moses, saying, 'If you are unfaithful, I will scatter you among the peoples; but if you return to me and keep my commandments and do them, though your dispersed be under the farthest skies, I will gather them thence and bring them to the place which I have chosen, to make my name dwell there.' They are thy servants and thy people, whom thou hast redeemed by thy great power and by thy strong hand. O Lord, let thy ear be attentive to the prayer of thy servant, and to the prayer of thy servants who delight to fear thy name; and give success to thy servant today, and grant him mercy in the sight of this man."

Tobias's Prayer, Tobit 8:4-8

When the door was shut and the two were alone, Tobias got up from the bed and said [to his wife], "Sister, get up, and let us pray that the Lord may have mercy upon us." And Tobias began to pray,

"Blessed art thou, O God of our fathers,
  and blessed be thy holy and glorious name for ever.
  Let the heavens and all thy creatures bless thee.
Thou madest Adam and gavest him Eve his wife
  as a helper and support.
  From them the race of mankind has sprung.
Thou didst say, 'It is not good that the man should be alone;
  let us make a helper for him like himself.'
And now, O Lord, I am not taking this sister of mine because of lust, but with sincerity. Grant that I may find mercy and may grow old together with her." And she said with him, "Amen."

Esther's Prayer, Esther 14:3-19
Queen Esther pleading before the King for her people is viewed as a type of Mary as the Queen of Heaven pleading before God on our behalf.

"O my Lord, thou only art our King; help me, who am alone and have no helper but thee, for my danger is in my hand. Ever since I was born I have heard in the tribe of my family that thou, O Lord, didst take Israel out of all the nations, and our fathers from among all their ancestors, for an everlasting inheritance, and that thou didst do for them all that thou didst promise. And now we have sinned before thee, and thou hast given us into the hands of our enemies, because we glorified their gods. Thou art righteous, O Lord! And now they are not satisfied that we are in bitter slavery, but they have covenanted with their idols to abolish what thy mouth has ordained and to destroy thy inheritance, to stop the mouths of those who praise thee and to quench thy altar and the glory of thy house, to open the mouths of the nations for the praise of vain idols, and to magnify for ever a mortal king. O Lord, do not surrender thy scepter to what has no being; and do not let them mock at our downfall; but turn their plan against themselves, and make an example of the man who began this against us. Remember, O Lord; make thyself known in this time of our affliction, and give me courage, O King of the gods and Master of all dominion! Put eloquent speech in my mouth before the lion, and turn his heart to hate the man who is fighting against us, so that there may be an end of him and those who agree with him. But save us by thy hand, and help me, who am alone and have no helper but thee, O Lord. …, and I have not honored the king's feast or drunk the wine of the libations. Thy servant has had no joy since the day that I was brought here until now, except in thee, O Lord God of Abraham. O God, whose might is over all, hear the voice of the despairing, and save us from the hands of evildoers. And save me from my fear!"

A Selection of Psalms
What follows is only a brief selection of Psalms on the theme of praying for God's mercy. There are many other Psalms on praying for God's mercy and on the related theme of trusting in God. Depending upon the particular translation of the Bible, mercy is sometimes rendered as "steadfast love" or loving-kindness."

Psalm 4 (Revised Grail Psalter)

2
    I called, the God of justice gave me answer;
    from anguish you released me, have mercy and hear me!

3
    Children of man, how long will my glory be dishonored,
    will you love what is futile and seek what is false?

4
    Know that the LORD works wonders for his faithful one;
    the LORD will hear me whenever I call him.

5
    Tremble, do not sin: ponder on your bed and be still.

6
    Offer right sacrifice, and trust in the LORD.

7
    "What can bring us happiness?" many say.
    Lift up the light of your face on us, O LORD.

8
    You have put into my heart a greater joy
    than abundance of grain and new wine can provide.

9
    In peace I will lie down and fall asleep,
    for you alone, O LORD, make me dwell in safety.

Psalm 6 (Revised Grail Psalter)

2
O LORD, do not rebuke me in your anger;
reprove me not in your rage.

3
Have mercy on me, LORD, for I languish.
LORD, heal me; my bones are shaking,

4
and my soul is greatly shaken.
But you, O LORD, how long?

5
Return, LORD, rescue my soul.
Save me in your merciful love.

6
For in death there is no remembrance of you;
from the grave, who can give you praise?

7
I am exhausted with my groaning;
every night I drench my bed with tears,
I bedew my couch with weeping.

8
My eyes waste away with grief;
I have grown old surrounded by all my foes.

9
Leave me, all who do evil,
for the LORD heeds the sound of my weeping.

10
The LORD has heard my plea;
the LORD will receive my prayer.

11
All my foes will be shamed and greatly shaken,
suddenly put to shame.

Psalm 51 (Revised Grail Psalter)
Known as the "Miserere," Psalm 51 is the Church's great pentitential psalm.

3
Have mercy on me, O God,
according to your merciful love;
according to your great compassion,
blot out my transgressions.

4
Wash me completely from my iniquity,
and cleanse me from my sin.

5
My transgressions, truly I know them;
my sin is always before me.

6
Against you, you alone, have I sinned;
what is evil in your sight I have done.
So you are just in your sentence,
without reproach in your judgment.

7
O see, in guilt I was born,
a sinner when my mother conceived me.

8
Yes, you delight in sincerity of heart;
in secret you teach me wisdom.

9
Cleanse me with hyssop, and I shall be pure;
wash me, and I shall be whiter than snow.

10
Let me hear rejoicing and gladness,
that the bones you have crushed may exult.

11
Turn away your face from my sins,
and blot out all my guilt.

12
Create a pure heart for me, O God;
renew a steadfast spirit within me.

13
Do not cast me away from your presence;
take not your holy spirit from me.

14
Restore in me the joy of your salvation;
sustain in me a willing spirit.

15
I will teach transgressors your ways,
that sinners may return to you.

16
Rescue me from bloodshed, O God,
God of my salvation,
and then my tongue shall ring out your justice.

17
O LORD, open my lips
and my mouth shall proclaim your praise.

18
For in sacrifice you take no delight;
burnt offering from me would not please you.

19
My sacrifice to God, a broken spirit:
a broken and humbled heart,
O God, you will not spurn.

20
In your good pleasure, show favor to Sion;
rebuild the walls of Jerusalem.

21
Then you will delight in right sacrifice,
burnt offerings wholly consumed.

Then you will be offered young bulls on your altar.

Psalm 89 (Revised Grail Psalter)

Psalm 89:2 was a favorite Scripture verse of Pope John Paul II, who would frequently recite it on important occasions during his papacy, such as the canonization of St. Faustina on April 30, 2000.

2
I will sing forever of your mercies, O LORD;
through all ages my mouth will proclaim your fidelity.

3
I have declared your mercy is established forever;
your fidelity stands firm as the heavens.

4
"With my chosen one I have made a covenant;
I have sworn to David my servant:

5
I will establish your descendants forever,
and set up your throne through all ages."

6
The heavens praise your wonders, O LORD,
your fidelity in the assembly of your holy ones.

7
For who in the skies can compare with the LORD,
or who is like the LORD among the heavenly powers?

8
A God to be feared in the council of the holy ones,
great and awesome to all around him.

9
O LORD God of hosts, who is your equal?
You are mighty, O LORD, and fidelity surrounds you.

10
It is you who rule the raging of the sea;
it is you who still the surging of its waves.

11
It is you who crush Rahab underfoot like a corpse;
you scatter your foes with your mighty arm.

12
> The heavens are yours, the earth is yours;
> you have founded the world and its fullness;

13
> it is you who created the North and the South.
> Tabor and Hermon shout for joy at your name.

14
> Yours is a mighty arm.
> Your hand is strong; your right hand is exalted.

15
> Justice and right judgment are the pillars of your throne;
> merciful love and fidelity walk in your presence.

16
> How blessed the people who know your praise,
> who walk, O LORD, in the light of your face,

17
> who find their joy every day in your name,
> who make your justice their joyful acclaim.

18
> For you are the glory of their strength;
> by your favor it is that our might is exalted.

19
> Behold, the LORD is our shield;
> he is the Holy One of Israel, our king.

20
> Then you spoke in a vision.
> To your faithful ones you said,
> "I have set the crown on a warrior,
> I have exalted one chosen from the people.

21
> I have found my servant David,
> and with my holy oil anointed him.

22
> My hand shall always be with him,
> and my arm shall make him strong.

23
> The enemy shall never outwit him,
> nor shall the son of iniquity humble him.

24
> I will beat down his foes before him,
> and those who hate him I will strike.

25
> My mercy and my faithfulness shall be with him;
> by my name his might shall be exalted.

26
I will stretch out his hand to the Sea,
and his right hand upon the Rivers.

27
He will call out to me, 'You are my father,
my God, the rock of my salvation.'

28
I for my part will make him my firstborn,
the highest of the kings of the earth.

29
will keep my faithful love for him always;
with him my covenant shall last.

30
I will establish his descendants forever,
and his throne as lasting as the days of heaven.

31
If his descendants forsake my law
and refuse to walk as I decree,

32
and if ever they violate my statutes,
failing to keep my commands:

33
Then I will punish their offenses with the rod;
then I will scourge them on account of their guilt.

34
But I will never take back my mercy;
my fidelity will never fail.

35
I will never violate my covenant,
nor go back on the promise of my lips.

36
Once for all, I have sworn by my holiness.
'I will never lie to David.

37
His descendants shall continue forever.
In my sight his throne is like the sun;

38
like the moon, it shall endure forever,
a faithful witness in the heavens.'"

39
But yet you have spurned and rejected,
you are angry with the one you have anointed.

40
You have renounced your covenant with your servant,
and dishonored his crown in the dust.

41

  You have broken down all his walls,
  and reduced his fortresses to ruins.

42

  All who pass by despoil him;
  he has become the taunt of his neighbors.

43

  You have exalted the right hand of his foes;
  you have made all his enemies rejoice.

44

  You have turned back the edge of his sword;
  you have not upheld him in battle.

45

  You have brought his glory to an end;
  you have hurled his throne to the ground.

46

  You have cut short the days of his youth;
  you have heaped disgrace upon him.

47

  How long, O LORD? Will you hide yourself forever?
  How long will your anger burn like a fire?

48

  Remember the shortness of my life,
  and how frail you have made the children of men.

49

  What man can live and never see death?
  Who can save himself from the grasp of the tomb?

50

  Where are your mercies of the past, O LORD,
  which you swore in your faithfulness to David?

51

  Remember, O LORD, the taunts to your servant,
  how I have to bear all the insults of the peoples.

52

  Thus your enemies lift up a taunt, O LORD,
  taunting your anointed at every step.

53

  Blest be the LORD forever.

  Amen and amen!

Jeremiah 14:7-9

"Though our iniquities testify against us,
  act, O Lord, for thy name's sake;
for our backslidings are many,
  we have sinned against thee.
O thou hope of Israel,
  its savior in time of trouble,
why shouldst thou be like a stranger in the land,
  like a wayfarer who turns aside to tarry for a night?
Why shouldst thou be like a man confused,
  like a mighty man who cannot save?
Yet thou, O Lord, art in the midst of us,
  and we are called by thy name;
  leave us not."

Lamentations 3:19-42

Remember my affliction and my bitterness,
  the wormwood and the gall!
My soul continually thinks of it
  and is bowed down within me.
But this I call to mind,
  and therefore I have hope:
The steadfast love of the Lord never ceases,
  his mercies never come to an end;
they are new every morning;
  great is thy faithfulness.
"The Lord is my portion," says my soul,
  "therefore I will hope in him."
The Lord is good to those who wait for him,
  to the soul that seeks him.
It is good that one should wait quietly
  for the salvation of the Lord.
It is good for a man that he bear
  the yoke in his youth.
Let him sit alone in silence
  when he has laid it on him;
let him put his mouth in the dust —
  there may yet be hope;
let him give his cheek to the smiter,

and be filled with insults.
For the Lord will not
  cast off for ever,
but, though he cause grief, he will have compassion
  according to the abundance of his steadfast love;
for he does not willingly afflict
  or grieve the sons of men.
To crush under foot
  all the prisoners of the earth,
to turn aside the right of a man
  in the presence of the Most High,
to subvert a man in his cause,
  the Lord does not approve.
Who has commanded and it came to pass,
  unless the Lord has ordained it?
Is it not from the mouth of the Most High
  that good and evil come?
Why should a living man complain,
  a man, about the punishment of his sins?
Let us test and examine our ways,
  and return to the Lord!
Let us lift up our hearts and hands
  to God in heaven:
"We have transgressed and rebelled,
  and thou hast not forgiven."

Baruch 2:11-19

"And now, O Lord God of Israel, who didst bring thy people out of the land of Egypt with a mighty hand and with signs and wonders and with great power and outstretched arm, and hast made thee a name, as at this day, we have sinned, we have been ungodly, we have done wrong, O Lord our God, against all thy ordinances. Let thy anger turn away from us, for we are left, few in number, among the nations where thou hast scattered us. Hear, O Lord, our prayer and our supplication, and for thy own sake deliver us, and grant us favor in the sight of those who have carried us into exile; that all the earth may know that thou art the Lord our God, for Israel and his descendants are called by thy name. O Lord, look down from thy holy habitation, and consider us. Incline thy ear, O Lord, and hear; open thy eyes, O

Lord, and see; for the dead who are in Hades, whose spirit has been taken from their bodies, will not ascribe glory or justice to the Lord, but the person that is greatly distressed, that goes about bent over and feeble, and the eyes that are failing, and the person that hungers, will ascribe to thee glory and righteousness, O Lord. For it is not because of any righteous deeds of our fathers or our kings that we bring before thee our prayer for mercy, O Lord our God."

Baruch 3:1-8

"O Lord Almighty, God of Israel, the soul in anguish and the wearied spirit cry out to thee. Hear, O Lord, and have mercy, for we have sinned before thee. For thou art enthroned for ever, and we are perishing for ever. O Lord Almighty, God of Israel, hear now the prayer of the dead of Israel and of the sons of those who sinned before thee, who did not heed the voice of the Lord their God, so that calamities have clung to us. Remember not the iniquities of our fathers, but in this crisis remember thy power and thy name. For thou art the Lord our God, and thee, O Lord, will we praise. For thou hast put the fear of thee in our hearts in order that we should call upon thy name; and we will praise thee in our exile, for we have put away from our hearts all the iniquity of our fathers who sinned before thee. Behold, we are today in our exile where thou hast scattered us, to be reproached and cursed and punished for all the iniquities of our fathers who forsook the Lord our God.'"

Daniel 3:16-22

Yet with a contrite heart and a humble spirit may we be accepted,
 as though it were with burnt offerings of rams and bulls,
 and with tens of thousands of fat lambs;
such may our sacrifice be in thy sight this day,
 and may we wholly follow thee,
 for there will be no shame for those who trust in thee.
And now with all our heart we follow thee,
 we fear thee and seek thy face.
Do not put us to shame,
 but deal with us in thy forbearance

and in thy abundant mercy.
Deliver us in accordance with thy marvelous works,
  and give glory to thy name, O Lord!
Let all who do harm to thy servants be put to shame;
let them be disgraced and deprived of all power and dominion,
  and let their strength be broken.
Let them know that thou art the Lord, the only God,
  glorious over the whole world."

Daniel 3:67-68

"Give thanks to the Lord, for he is good,
    for his mercy endures for ever.
Bless him, all who worship the Lord, the God of gods,
    sing praise to him and give thanks to him,
    for his mercy endures for ever."

Habbakuk 3:2

O Lord, I have heard the report of thee,
  and thy work, O Lord, do I fear.
In the midst of the years renew it;
  in the midst of the years make it known;
  in wrath remember mercy.

The Our Father, Matthew 6:9-13
The call to forgiveness is at the heart of the most important prayer that Jesus gave us.

"Our Father who art in heaven,
Hallowed be thy name.
Thy kingdom come,
Thy will be done,
  On earth as it is in heaven.
Give us this day our daily bread;
And forgive us our debts,
  As we also have forgiven our debtors;
And lead us not into temptation,
  But deliver us from evil."

Mary's Magnificat, Luke 1:46-55

Using the Magnificat as his principal source, Pope John Paul II devoted an entire section (9) to Mary as "Mother of Mercy" in his encyclical Rich in Mercy.

"My soul magnifies the Lord,
and my spirit rejoices in God my Savior,
for he has regarded the low estate of his handmaiden.
For behold, henceforth all generations will call me blessed;
for he who is mighty has done great things for me,
and holy is his name.
And his mercy is on those who fear him from generation
to generation.
He has shown strength with his arm,
he has scattered the proud in the imagination of their hearts,
he has put down the mighty from their thrones,
and exalted those of low degree;
he has filled the hungry with good things,
and the rich he has sent empty away.
He has helped his servant Israel,
in remembrance of his mercy,
as he spoke to our fathers,
to Abraham and to his posterity for ever."

Luke 18:13

In Jesus' parable of the Pharisee and the tax collector in the Temple, this is the honest, heartfelt prayer of the tax collector

"God, be merciful to me a sinner!"

Luke 23:34

This is the prayer of Jesus from the Cross for those who were crucifying Him.

"Father, forgive them; for they know not what they do."

PRAYERS *from* *the* DIARY OF SAINT FAUSTINA

A short prayer Jesus taught St. Faustina

"Jesus, I trust in You!" (*Diary*, 47). *It is the shortest Divine Mercy prayer that has spread around the world, and it appears on every image of The Divine Mercy. Trust in Jesus is the summary of the message of Divine Mercy.*

Prayer for the Conversion of Sinners

Jesus said to St. Faustina:

You always console Me when you pray for sinners. The prayer most pleasing to Me is the prayer for the conversion of sinners. Know, My daughter, that this prayer is always heard and answered (*Diary*, 1397).

On another occasion, He told her:

I desire that you know more profoundly the love that burns in My Heart for souls, and you will understand this when you meditate upon My Passion. Call upon My mercy on behalf of sinners; I desire their salvation. When you say this prayer with a contrite heart and with faith on behalf of some sinner, I will give him the grace of conversion. This is the prayer:

"O Blood and Water, which gushed forth from the Heart of Jesus as a fountain of mercy for us, I trust in You" (*Diary*, 186, 187).

This promise of our Lord was specifically made to St. Faustina, but if we pray this prayer with the same purity of intention, we have reason to believe God will honor it.

Short Exclamatory Prayers

Most Merciful Heart of Jesus, protect us from the just anger of God (*Diary*, 1526).

O Christ, although much effort is required, all things can be done with Your grace (*Diary*, 1696).

O my Jesus, I am making at this very moment a firm and eternal resolution by virtue of Your grace and mercy, fidelity to the tiniest grace of Yours (*Diary*, 716).

With Jesus, through Jesus and in Jesus is my communion with You, Eternal Father (*Diary*, 648).

O my God, I love You (*Diary*, 1323).

King of Mercy, guide my soul (*Diary*, 3).

Jesus, I trust in You; I trust in the ocean of Your mercy. You are a Mother to me (*Diary*, 249).

O my God, my only hope, I have placed all my trust in You, and I know I shall not be disappointed (*Diary*, 317).

O purest Love, rule in all Your plenitude in my heart and help me to do Your holy will most faithfully! (*Diary*, 328).

Jesus, Life and Truth, my Master, guide every step of my life, that I may act according to Your holy will (*Diary*, 688).

My Jesus, my strength and my only hope, in You alone is all my hope. My trust will not be frustrated (*Diary*, 746).

O Jesus, have mercy! Embrace the whole world and press me to Your Heart ... O Lord, let my soul repose in the sea of Your unfathomable mercy (*Diary*, 869).

Hide me, Jesus, in the depths of Your mercy, and then let my neighbor judge me as he pleases (*Diary*, 791).

O Jesus, shield me with Your mercy and also judge me leniently, or else Your justice may rightly damn me (*Diary*, 1093).

The Chaplet of Divine Mercy

You will recite it for nine days, on the beads of the rosary, in the following manner: First of all, you will say one OUR FATHER and HAIL MARY and the I BELIEVE IN GOD. Then on the OUR FATHER beads you will say the following words: "Eternal Father, I offer You the Body and Blood, Soul and Divinity of Your dearly beloved Son, Our Lord Jesus Christ, in atonement for our sins and those of the whole world." On the HAIL MARY beads you will say the following words: "For the sake of His sorrowful Passion have mercy on us and on the whole world." In conclusion, three times you will recite these words: "Holy God, Holy Mighty One, Holy Immortal One, have mercy on us and on the whole world" (*Diary*, 476).

Prayers on the Call to Be Merciful

O Most Holy Trinity! As many times as I breathe, as many times as my heart beats, as many times as my blood pulsates through my body, so many thousand times do I want to glorify Your mercy.

I want to be completely transformed into Your mercy and to be Your living reflection, O Lord. May the greatest of all divine attributes, that of Your unfathomable mercy, pass through my heart and soul to my neighbor.

Help me, O Lord, that my eyes may be merciful, so that I may never suspect or judge from appearances, but look for what is beautiful in my neighbors' souls and come to their rescue.

Help me, that my ears may be merciful, so that I may give heed to my neighbors' needs and not be indifferent to their pains and moanings.

Help me, O Lord, that my tongue may be merciful, so that I should never speak negatively of my neighbor, but have a word of comfort and forgiveness for all.

Help me, O Lord, that my hands may be merciful and filled with good deeds, so that I may do only good to my neighbors and take upon myself the more difficult and toilsome tasks.

Help me, that my feet may be merciful, so that I may hurry to assist my neighbor, overcoming my own fatigue and weariness. My true rest is in the service of my neighbor.

Help me, O Lord, that my heart may be merciful so that I myself may feel all the sufferings of my neighbor. I will refuse my heart to no one. I will be sincere even with those who, I know, will abuse my kindness. And I will lock myself up in the most merciful Heart of Jesus. I will bear my own suffering in silence. May Your mercy, O Lord, rest upon me.

You Yourself command me to exercise the three degrees of mercy. The first: the act of mercy, of whatever kind. The second: the word of mercy — if I cannot carry out a work of mercy, I will assist by my words. The third: prayer — if I cannot show mercy by deeds or words, I can always do so by prayer. My prayer reaches out even there where I cannot reach out physically.

O my Jesus, transform me into Yourself, for You can do all things (*Diary*, 163).

O my Jesus, teach me to open the bosom of mercy and love to everyone who asks for it. Jesus, my Commander, teach me so that all my prayers and deeds may bear the seal of Your mercy (*Diary*, 755).

O Jesus, I understand that Your mercy is beyond all imagining, and therefore I ask You to make my heart so big that there will be room in it for the needs of all the souls living on the face of the earth. O Jesus, my love extends beyond the world, to the souls suffering in purgatory, and I want to exercise mercy toward them by means of indulgenced prayers. God's mercy is unfathomable and inexhaustible, just as God himself is unfathomable. Even if I were to use the strongest words there are to express this mercy of God, all this would be nothing in comparison with what it is in reality. O Jesus, make my heart sensitive to all the sufferings of my neighbor, whether of body or of soul. O my Jesus, I know that You act toward us as we act toward our neighbor.

My Jesus, make my heart like unto Your merciful Heart. Jesus, help me to go through life doing good to everyone (*Diary*, 692).

Prayer for Mercy on the Whole World
This prayer is used daily at the National Shrine of The Divine Mercy, Stockbridge, Massachusetts.

O greatly merciful God, Infinite Goodness, today all mankind calls out from the abyss of its misery to Your mercy — to Your compassion, O God; and it is with its mighty voice of misery that it cries out. Gracious God, do not reject the prayer of this earth's exiles! O Lord, Goodness beyond our understanding, who are acquainted with our misery through and through, and know that by our own power we cannot ascend to You, we implore You; anticipate us with Your grace and keep on increasing Your mercy in us, that we may faithfully do Your holy will all through our life and at death's hour. Let the omnipotence of Your mercy shield us from the darts of our salvation's enemies, that we may with confidence, as Your children, await Your final coming — that day known to You alone. And we expect to obtain everything promised us by Jesus in spite of all our wretchedness. For Jesus is our Hope: Through His merciful Heart, as through an open gate, we pass through to heaven (*Diary*, 1570).

Saint Faustina's Litany of Praises to Divine Mercy

Let the doubting soul read these considerations on Divine Mercy and become trusting.
Divine Mercy, gushing forth from the bosom of the Father,
    I trust in You.
Divine Mercy, greatest attribute of God, I trust in You.
Divine Mercy, incomprehensible mystery, I trust in You.
Divine Mercy, fountain gushing forth from the mystery of the
    Most Blessed Trinity, I trust in You.
Divine Mercy, unfathomed by any intellect, human or angelic,
    I trust in You.
Divine Mercy, from which wells forth all life and happiness,
    I trust in You.
Divine Mercy, better than the heavens, I trust in You.
Divine Mercy, source of miracles and wonders, I trust in You.
Divine Mercy, encompassing the whole universe, I trust in You.
Divine Mercy, descending to earth in the Person of the Incarnate
    Word, I trust in You.

Divine Mercy, which flowed out from the open wound of the
  Heart of Jesus, I trust in You.
Divine Mercy, enclosed in the Heart of Jesus for us, and especially
  for sinners, I trust in You.
Divine Mercy, unfathomed in the institution of the Sacred Host,
  I trust in You.
Divine Mercy, in the founding of Holy Church, I trust in You.
Divine Mercy, in the Sacrament of Holy Baptism, I trust in You.
Divine Mercy, in our justification through Jesus Christ,
  I trust in You.
Divine Mercy, accompanying us through our whole life,
  I trust in You.
Divine Mercy, embracing us especially at the hour of death,
  I trust in You.
Divine Mercy, endowing us with immortal life, I trust in You.
Divine Mercy, accompanying us every moment of our life,
  I trust in You.
Divine Mercy, shielding us from the fire of hell, I trust in You.
Divine Mercy, in the conversion of hardened sinners,
  I trust in You.
Divine Mercy, astonishment for Angels, incomprehensible to
  Saints, I trust in You.
Divine Mercy, unfathomed in all the mysteries of God,
  I trust in You.
Divine Mercy, lifting us out of every misery, I trust in You.
Divine Mercy, source of our happiness and joy, I trust in You.
Divine Mercy, in calling us forth from nothingness to
  existence, I trust in You.
Divine Mercy, embracing all the works of His hands,
  I trust in You.
Divine Mercy, crown of all of God's handiwork, I trust in You.
Divine Mercy, in which we are all immersed, I trust in You.
Divine Mercy, sweet relief for anguished hearts, I trust in You.
Divine Mercy, only hope of despairing souls, I trust in You.
Divine Mercy, repose of hearts, peace amidst fear,
  I trust in You.
Divine Mercy, delight and ecstasy of holy souls, I trust in You.
Divine Mercy, inspiring hope against all hope, I trust in You.

Eternal God, in whom mercy is endless and the treasury of
compassion inexhaustible, look kindly upon us and increase

Your mercy in us, that in difficult moments we might not despair nor become despondent, but with great confidence submit ourselves to Your holy will, which is Love and Mercy itself (*Diary*, 949-50).

Prayer for Priests

O my Jesus, I beg You on behalf of the whole Church: Grant it love and the light of Your Spirit and give power to the words of priests so that hardened hearts might be brought to repentance and return to You, O Lord. Lord, give us holy priests; You Yourself maintain them in holiness. O Divine and Great High Priest, may the power of Your mercy accompany them everywhere and protect them from the devil's traps and snares which are continually being set for the souls of priests. May the power of Your mercy, O Lord, shatter and bring to naught all that might tarnish the sanctity of priests, for You can do all things (*Diary*, 1052). I ask You for a special blessing and for light, O Jesus, for the priests before whom I will make my confessions throughout my lifetime (*Diary*, 240).

Prayer in Time of Suffering

Jesus, do not leave me alone in suffering. You know, Lord, how weak I am. I am an abyss of wretchedness, I am nothingness itself; so what will be so strange if You leave me alone and I fall? I am an infant, Lord, so I cannot get along by myself. However, beyond all abandonment I trust, and in spite of my own feeling I trust, and I am being completely transformed into trust — often in spite of what I feel. Do not lessen any of my sufferings, only give me strength to bear them. Do with me as You please, Lord, only give me the grace to be able to love You in every event and circumstance. Lord, do not lessen my cup of bitterness, only give me strength that I may be able to drink it all (*Diary*, 1489).

Prayer at the Feet of the Eucharist

O Jesus, Divine Prisoner of Love, when I consider Your love and how You emptied Yourself for me, my senses fail me. You hide Your inconceivable majesty and lower Yourself to miserable me. O King of Glory, though You hide Your beauty, yet the eye of my soul rends the veil. I see the angelic choirs giving You honor without cease, and all the heavenly Powers praising You without cease, and without cease they are saying: Holy, Holy, Holy.

Oh, who will comprehend Your love and Your unfathomable mercy toward us! O Prisoner of Love, I lock up my poor heart in this tabernacle that it may adore You without cease night and day. I know of no obstacle in this adoration, and even though I be physically distant, my heart is always with You. Nothing can put a stop to my love for You. No obstacles exist for me (*Diary*, 80).

O Holy Trinity, One and Indivisible God, may You be blessed for this great gift and testament of mercy (*Diary*, 81).

I adore You, Lord and Creator, hidden in the Blessed Sacrament. I adore You for all the works of Your hands, that reveal to me so much wisdom, goodness and mercy, O Lord. You have spread so much beauty over the earth, and it tells me about Your beauty, even though these beautiful things are but a faint reflection of You, Incomprehensible Beauty. And although You have hidden Yourself and concealed Your beauty, my eye, enlightened by faith, reaches You, and my soul recognizes its Creator, its Highest good; and my heart is completely immersed in prayer of adoration (*Diary*, 1692).

My Lord and Creator, Your goodness encourages me to converse with You. Your mercy abolishes the chasm which separates the Creator from the creature. To converse with You, O Lord, is the delight of my heart. In You I find everything that my heart could desire. Here Your light illumines my mind, enabling it to know You more and more deeply. Here streams of graces flow down upon my heart. Here my soul draws eternal life. O my Lord and Creator, You alone, beyond all these gifts, give Your own self to me and unite Yourself intimately with Your miserable creature (*Diary*, 1692).

ABOUT THE AUTHOR

Known to many as "the man who sings the Divine Mercy Chaplet on EWTN," this father of seven has been involved in a ministry of mercy for over 45 years, using his gifts of teaching, writing, counseling, music, and prayer to help people understand the teachings of the Church and open their hearts to the healing touch of God's love.

As a teacher and counselor for 14 years, Vinny experienced firsthand how much healing is needed in the world. Feeling called to respond to this need, he began using his gifts in full-time religious ministry. His powerful teachings on Divine Mercy, Mary, the Sacraments, and the Father's love have made him a popular speaker at parish missions, conferences, and retreats.

A former executive editor at the Marian Helpers Center and former general manager of Divine Mercy International, Vinny was actively involved in spreading the message of Divine Mercy, presenting workshops for clergy, religious, and lay leaders, and writing or editing various Divine Mercy publications, including the official English edition of the *Diary of St. Maria Faustina Kowalska: Divine Mercy in My Soul*. His personal, straightforward style of writing makes theological concepts and the teachings of the Church come alive with new meaning and relevancy.

Co-author of *The Divine Mercy Message and Devotion* and *Now Is the Time for Mercy*, Vinny has also published articles in various Catholic periodicals, including *Catholic Digest, Legatus, Queen, Columbia, Marian Helper*, and the *Friends of Mercy* newsletter. His bestselling books include *7 Secrets of the Eucharist*, (over 100,000 copies sold), *7 Secrets of Confession*, and *21 Ways to Worship*.

Vinny is currently director of MercySong, a family-based 501(c)(3) Catholic not-for-profit ministry dedicated to bringing healing to others by leading them to a personal experience of the Father's love through music, teaching, writing, counseling, and prayer.

PROMOTING DIVINE MERCY SINCE 1941

Marian Press, the publishing apostolate of the Marian Fathers of the Immaculate Conception of the B.V.M., has published and distributed millions of religious books, magazines, and pamphlets that teach, encourage, and edify Catholics around the world. Our publications promote and support the ministry and spirituality of the Marians worldwide. Loyal to the Holy Father and to the teachings of the Catholic Church, the Marians fulfill their special mission by:

- Fostering devotion to Mary, the Immaculate Conception.
- Promoting the Divine Mercy message and devotion.
- Offering assistance to the dying and the deceased, especially the victims of war and disease.
- Promoting Christian knowledge, administering parishes, shrines, and conducting missions.

Based in Stockbridge, Mass., Marian Press is known as the publisher of the *Diary of Saint Maria Faustina Kowalska*, and the Marians are the leading authorities on the Divine Mercy message and devotion.

Stockbridge is also the home of the National Shrine of The Divine Mercy, the Association of Marian Helpers, and a destination for thousands of pilgrims each year.

Globally, the Marians' ministries also include missions in developing countries where the spiritual and material needs are enormous.

To learn more about the Marians, their spirituality, publications or ministries, visit **marian.org** or **thedivinemercy.org**, the Marians' website that is devoted exclusively to Divine Mercy.

Below is a view of the National Shrine of The Divine Mercy and its Residence in Stockbridge, Mass. The Shrine, which was built in the 1950s, was declared a National Shrine by the National Conference of Catholic Bishops on March 20, 1996.

© MARIE ROMAGNANO

Visit us at the National Shrine of The Divine Mercy in Stockbridge, Mass.
For more information: thedivinemercy.org/shrine or 413-298-1118.

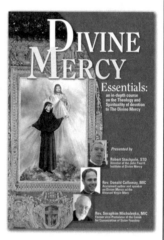
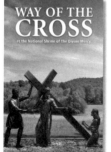

DIVINE MERCY RESOURCES

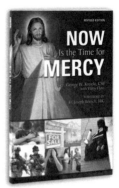

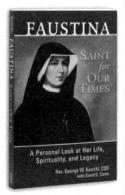

MORE TITLES BY VINNY FLYNN

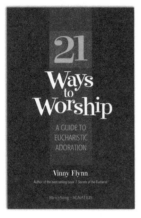

21 WAYS TO WORSHIP
A GUIDE TO EUCHARISTIC ADORATION

From Vinny Flynn, bestselling author of *7 Secrets of the Eucharist*, comes this easy-to-read, practical guide, jam-packed with inspiring ideas, techniques, and prayers to help you make the most of your time in Adoration. It's a perfect resource for the beginner wondering what Adoration is all about, and for the veteran adorer looking for additional ideas. 162 pages. **21WTW   9781884479441**

7 SECRETS OF THE EUCHARIST

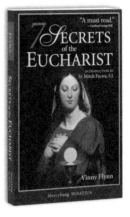

Get ready to discover the "hidden" truths of the Holy Eucharist – truths embraced by theologians, saints, and mystics — now finally made understandable to all. Author Vinny Flynn provides a new understanding of the Mass, the way Jesus is present in this Sacrament, and a new awareness that the Eucharist is not just about receiving Communion. It's also about transforming your daily life. Soft cover. 131 pages. 7 1/2" x 4 3/4".
SOTE 9781884479311
Companion resources: Study Guide: 6" x 9". 88 pages. SG7S
DVD: 67 minutes. 7SDVD Audiobook: 1 hr., 49 min. 7SAB

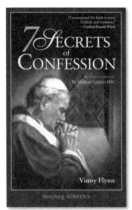

7 SECRETS OF CONFESSION

Author Vinny Flynn unveils 7 key "secrets" or hidden truths about the great spiritual beauty, power, and depth of Confession. If you have not yet experienced Confession as a wonderful, personal encounter with Christ; if you do not yet look forward to going to Confession with the same eagerness and expectation with which you receive Holy Communion, this book is for you. It will be a whole new way of going to Confession, inviting you to begin an exciting personal journey to healing and holiness. It may change your life. Paperback. 200 pages.

7SOC   9781884479465

Also from MercySong

ROSARY AND CHAPLET

This bestselling MercySong album includes recited versions of the Holy Rosary and the Chaplet of Divine Mercy with powerful meditations on the Passion from St. Faustina's *Diary*. 40 minutes. **CD: RCMCD 9781884479154**

These MercySong products are distributed by Marian Press.